# DANCE TO SUCCESS

# DANCE TO SUCCESS

## DANCE BECAUSE YOU CAN!

Moshe A. Rasier

ISBN: 0692677852
ISBN 13: 9780692677858
Library of Congress Control Number: 2016905332
DTS Publishing, Miami, FL

*I would like to dedicate this book to my ultimate mentor, my father; my family and the entire ADC family; as well as Lisa Jeffery, who encouraged me to write and publish it.*

*Dance because you can!*

—MOSHE RASIER, A.K.A. MR. CRUISE GUY

# The ADC Story

*It's kind of fun to do the impossible.*

—Walt Disney

Often people have asked me about my story, my background, and how my company, Aventura Dance Cruise (ADC), came to be. Usually I give people a short, two- or three-minute version of the basics. I mean, I don't find it that interesting—'cause I'm just another guy who's trying to make it in life, just like everyone else, right? I never considered myself to be a role model or someone people would look up to.

At first, it was humbling and touching to see a few people get inspired by my story, but after a while, I realized there was much more to it. Many people wanted to hear more. It seems like I do indeed inspire and encourage people to go after their goals. So, little by little, the idea of writing this book came about.

Growing up, I wasn't exactly a model student. In fact, to be honest, I was something of a clown. You could always find me bouncing around with my friends, playing soccer, or hanging at the beach, doing my best to stay out of trouble.

By the time I got to high school, I already had the clear sense that I was interested in business, interested in making money—why not? But I didn't know exactly what that meant or where it might lead me. Just the same, I carried a fantasy of myself wearing a suit, carrying a briefcase, and walking into an office every day. The problem was I had this vague sense that to make that fantasy into a reality, I would actually have to get good grades—which I most certainly did not. Yet I did major in business throughout high school, which was as serious a reflection of my intentions as I could point to.

Being the son of two immigrants, I was exposed to a unique mix of cultures. My mom is Argentinian, and my dad is Turkish with Spanish descent. And as for me, I grew up in the State of Israel. After high school in Israel, there is a period of mandatory military service. It's three years for men and a bit less than two years for women. Unless you have some medical condition that prohibits you from doing so, you have to serve. So right after high school, off I went.

Now, at the time, you didn't know whether or not you had graduated from high school (and received a *bagrut*, or diploma) until some months after the fact. It wasn't like in the United States, where you find out quickly and then go on to have a ceremony in which you're awarded your diploma in front of a crowd. So when I got the call about my graduation status, I really wasn't even thinking about it. I was busy attending to my army duties and kind of expecting that I hadn't graduated high school.

However, when that phone call came, the news was actually good! Against all odds, I'd done it! My diploma was there waiting for me. It wasn't as though I'd fully expected to fail, but I absolutely had not taken this news for granted in advance.

That left my future a bit more open. Meanwhile, I still had my obligation to the army. On one level, this made for wasted time. Unless you are looking ahead to a military future, those mandatory years of service are hardly essential. At the same time, the training in my first year of service taught me a lot. I learned time management. I learned how to face challenges. I developed a dependable sense of discipline. I found myself growing organized, independent, and accustomed to functioning at a high level in various locations.

It was certainly a marked contrast to the soccer-loving, beach-hitting social butterfly that I'd always been. Little by little, at my own pace and in my own way, I was actually becoming something new: a grown-up.

When I finally finished my mandatory service, I entered the job market for the first time in my life. Before I knew it, I hit my family and friends with a major two-tiered surprise: I was going to take off for a trip to Miami, Florida, and I was intent upon checking out some colleges over there.

In other words, this would be more than just a trip. It was my first visit to the United States, the doorway to my future. The location was as surprising to people as my pursuit of college ("Moshe? College? New country? Alone? New language?"), but I felt determined about the direction in which I was headed.

When I went to college in America—for both my bachelor's and my master's—I was a different kind of student than I had been in high school: focused, committed, and serious. All the while, I nurtured a dream of working in corporate America. I'd be wearing a classy suit and tie. I'd walk into work and be greeted by a secretary. All day long, I'd work the phones and computers, making important deals and making big things happen.

Little did I know how far that fantasy was from what would become my reality.

For starters, I found the process of searching for employment to be demeaning. There I was, with all the education, knowledge, and qualifications an employer could want, and time and time again, I found myself getting rejected. It was grueling for me to go out there and sell myself to people who had the power to determine my fate. I had this nagging sense that I should be the one in charge of determining my own fate.

*Some of us think holding on makes us*
*strong; but sometimes it is letting go.*

—HERMANN HESSE

Still, I eventually worked in corporate America at a couple of different jobs. But it didn't take long for me to realize that it was not for me. In the jobs I held, you went in, carried out your duties, clocked out at five o'clock, and then went home and forgot about it, only to do the exact same thing the following day. To say it was boring would be putting it mildly. And beyond being boring, it just seemed so insignificant to me. This is not a judgment on what anyone else does for a living, but I needed a greater sense of motion and purpose. I wanted to leave a mark on this world, to feel needed, and to help people rather than live as a cog in someone else's giant machine.

In other words, although I might not yet have had the word for it, I really wanted to be an entrepreneur.

Let's flash back to my college time for just a moment. I think on account of my army experience and my background, I didn't naturally gravitate toward other people my age. In my early twenties, I always made friends who were more mature than I was. I had a different background and mentality, one that somehow kept me at a distance from my peers. Most of my friends at the time were in relationships or married and owned businesses or had careers—you know, mature.

Little by little, I started catching hints from my circle of friends. Over and over, they kept suggesting that I should maybe go out and meet some people my own age. The first time this came up, I ignored it. The second time, I took mild notice. But after they repeated it a number of times, I finally got the message.

I had to branch out. It was for my own good.

So what could I do to kick-start my social life? Music had always been among my great loves, so I thought about taking music lessons, maybe to learn how to play the piano or guitar. But I realized that idea was just a stalling tactic. I mean, who would I meet while taking music lessons—the teacher?

No, to actually open up some kind of social circle, I would need to do something more daring.

I remembered an experience from high school when I had taken salsa-dancing lessons, and I recalled enjoying it. While my first lesson had been part of a date, I found myself going back for more lessons on my own, even though things didn't work out with the person I'd been dating. It was a fun activity—moving my body, getting the moves right—but not something that I might have expected to eventually define my existence.

I thought of perhaps going toward hip-hop dancing, which was supercool, but at the time, it was clearly far more geared toward young people. OK, I thought, then let's try Latin dancing.

Or, more specifically, salsa dancing!

I picked up the phone and called two schools. One didn't answer, but the other did. I scheduled my first class with the one that answered. Next thing I knew, I was going back for more instruction. I started as a beginner and then went on to intermediate, followed by advanced. I became good friends with the teachers. I had tons of fun.

I also joined a dance team.

Dance teams, as I would come to learn, make up their own culture. They consist of students performing dance routines in groups at events. For the performers, it's a great opportunity to learn and practice dancing on a whole new level. It's also simply exciting—to travel, to meet new people, to work with a talented team. In the Latin-dance industry, these teams are a staple. And as I got more into dance, I had the gratifying feeling of knowing I was part of something.

So the whole time I was at school with my head down, studying hard, and nailing down good grades, I was simultaneously living a second life as a dancer. For me, the key joy of being a dancer was simply having a way to get out there in the world. The art of dancing itself was one thing, but the pathway to people and experiences that dancing opened up for me was something else entirely.

I've found that in the world of dancing, in a single night, in a couple of hours, you can easily make more than twenty new friends—at least! For me, this was critical, as I had few friends to speak of elsewhere. There's even a term for it: social dancing. You can go to a social by yourself, but from the moment you walk in the door, you're not by yourself anymore. You walk in, throw on your dance shoes, grab a partner, and become part of the scene.

As I suffered behind my desk in corporate America, I realized more and more acutely that my dance hobby had been my single source of joy in recent years. How powerful that experience was and how it had changed my life! The contrast could not have been starker: behind a desk, I was a robot, while on the dance floor, I was energy in motion.

With this in mind, I decided to make my hobby my profession.

⟨⁓⟩

I opened up my own dance studio. What a risk! I'd never owned any business before, let alone a dance studio, and I hadn't studied dancing in school. I had no students whatsoever. I put 90 percent of the expenses on credit cards. (Mind you, I'm not recommending this tactic to others. I'm just saying that's what I did.) I asked questions. I found a spot, moved in, and hung a sign on the door:

Aventura Dance.

As I've explained, I had an understanding of dancing as both a social and a cultural phenomenon. Naming my dance studio after the city in which we operated was a calculated decision, as I was seeking to do more than open a school: I wanted to add to the prevailing culture. It was a lifestyle venue, created to give people experiences and to exist in a flow with the environment around us. Aventura, aside from being a city in Miami, means "adventure" in Spanish—and so it was!

All was well for a little while. The business was functioning at an OK level. But then a little thing happened in 2008 called the Great Recession.

Suddenly, I found myself blushing over my decision to launch a business on credit cards. The economy was in the gutter. Even under the best of circumstances, opening and sustaining a business is hard. There I was with the ground beneath my feet falling away.

I realized that even though I had a dance studio, dance lessons alone weren't enough to keep it going. So I threw parties. I offered private lessons. I even produced an instructional DVD. Meanwhile, the studio operated in a membership framework, in which the students paid a monthly fee. It remained important to me to do what I could to help create that sense of a dance lifestyle for my students. I didn't want anyone to be thinking about his or her money and payment every time he or she came to the studio. So as a part of the membership package, I came up with the idea of doing an annual location getaway with the members, so we could all go somewhere nice to do what we loved most—dance. It was a perfect combination of my goals of delivering a lifestyle and creating much-needed extra income.

As fate would have it, right next door to my dance studio was a travel agency. I'd always walk by it and see signs advertising cruises. I'd never been on a cruise before, but the idea of going spoke to me. Not only could we all be together in one place, but we could also actually be on *una aventura*—under one roof, with meals built in, and with the beautiful sight of the open ocean.

I connected with the travel agency and pitched the concept. They were completely up for it—after all, they wanted the business. The next day, we started weaving our plan together. I already had a nice database of students and prospective customers to work with.

At the time, social media more or less boiled down to Facebook, so I slapped an announcement on our Facebook page and our website:

Aventura Dance Cruise! Join the Adventure.
A weekend full of dance lessons and Latin music.
To sign up, go ahead and call this number...

Then I went ahead and forgot all about it.

The reason I did so was that this was only one small part of my business. My day-to-day activities were tied up with running the actual studio. It was July when I put up that initial Facebook post. The cruise itself wasn't set to take place until November.

Now, let me tell you about the power of social media and the Internet...

Little by little, I began to be contacted by different people, mostly friends of mine in the dance industry.

"Hey, I heard about your cruise. Sounds great. Can I bring my students, too?"

"Hey, do you mind if I teach some classes?"

"Hey, would like to bring me on as your deejay?"

"Hey, we have a new dance show—can we perform?"

Next thing I knew, I was adding this person to the roster and then that person. Then someone was bringing ten new friends, and another guy was bringing along his aunt Susan, and on and on and on.

This is not to say I expected us to have a smash hit on our hands. At most, in my wildest fantasies, I thought that maybe thirty or forty people would register. Maybe fifty, if the gods really smiled down on us. But I was hardly staking my future on the whole operation. I'd entrusted the travel agency with handling the bookings, and I kept my fingers crossed for a decent response.

Think about it: How many people could book a vacation and throw down money, just like that—in that economy?

A couple of weeks before the cruise, the travel agent gave me a call. "Hey, Moshe, are you excited? Are you ready?"

"Yeah, sure. I'm ready." What in the world was going on here? I wondered.

"Well, you better be ready," the agent went on to say. At which point, I heard a number that I will never forget in my whole life: 472. That's how many people had signed up!

My reality then became a blur.

On most levels, it was a dream come true. I'd had my breakthrough moment. I'd been delivered a great, golden gift from the gods of dance.

But let me point something out: you cannot possibly realize what "472 people" means until you see that many people standing in front of you, complete with the knowledge that you are the person responsible for their vacation.

We were as green as you could imagine. Fortunately, the cruise line was helpful, providing us with ample space. As for the trip itself, it was the epitome of a wild time. I could not even begin to summarize all the challenges, scenarios, and joys that it created. I cannot even recall sleeping for its duration. To this day, however, that initial voyage still gets referred to widely as a wonderful time, if not one of the best cruises to date.

After it was over, I said I'd never do it again, but upon recuperating, I came to my senses. I realized how much we'd touched people. So many photos, videos, and comments were all over Facebook, and so many e-mails poured in. We'd made so many people so happy, providing them with more than just a vacation. We'd given them an actual adventure, an escape from their everyday lives and the tough economic situation. I felt so fulfilled by the experience.

It was time to get organized and take this thing to the next level.

I came up with a precise plan. A detailed budget. I was more exacting. I knew far more about what to expect.

In our second year, we had seven hundred guests. In year three, the number was up to one thousand. And the growth just kept accumulating.

All of this, of course, sounds perfectly great, but I was in for a major lesson on the topic of growth.

As it turned out, in the cruise industry, small groups are beloved, but large groups are a problem. This is because, when the group gets too big, the cruise companies start to see it as a liability. I found that once our cruises had more than eight hundred people or so, I was treated differently. Even though I would have expected to be treated better, I apparently had too much power.

And power, as it turned out, has its downside.

The cruise companies started charging us new fees. More importantly, they started restricting us from all directions: less mobility, less usage of space, and less time to dance. The fees were so high and the restrictions so tough that they seemed designed to discourage me. There was no way in the world that I could overcome them.

So I decided that I'd had enough.

It had been a good run, but the party was over. From now on, we'd either be very small and exclusive, or perhaps there wouldn't even be any more cruises. In any case, I definitely didn't want to put a poor-quality product out there.

By then, I was a fixture in Miami's dance scene. On social media and at some local events, I started spreading the word: the next ADC would be our final one.

And the reaction was enough to break your heart.

"What?"

"How could you?"

"What are you thinking?"

People didn't understand where I was coming from. They just saw a guy pulling the plug on something new, fun, and exciting. Some even went so far as to suggest that this was a marketing move to get people to pay more or sign up faster. As much as I tried to explain, I couldn't make the message stick.

I wasn't just being met with disappointment; I was being met with protest.

That's when I realized how powerful this bonding experience was for so many people. It was a culture, a family.

It was ADC.

Then it occurred to me: What if, instead of depending on the cruise companies' regular cruises, we simply took over and booked the whole cruise? A full ship. Our own ship.

I started chatting about this with different travel experts, along with the cruise line's sales advisers. Needless to say, it would be an extremely serious operation. We'd need to know more than a travel agency about how cruises and the cruise industry actually worked. We'd need to know how to charge and price, how to manage the ship, and how to execute this whole humongous event. There was no book available at the library to walk me through the process step by step. I was one of very few people on earth undertaking such an endeavor. Forget about the stress or the many unknowns—I'd be on the hook for lots of money.

This was *huge*. This was impossible!

But wait! This was what I'd wanted back when I had been a corporate cog. And as much as I wanted to deny it, I've always been up for tackling a challenge.

So we did it: we booked a full-ship charter. We wouldn't be on *a* cruise; we'd be on *our* cruise. A full ship, just for us!

Our first full-ship voyage was in 2013. We had a lot of fun! It was so special, our first full-ship ADC! It was our first time doing it all, with no one there to tell us when, where, or how long to dance. We were in charge. We had two thousand captains. It was seventy-two hours of nonstop dancing. We learned a lot and took many notes for the following year.

The 2014 ADC was much, much improved. We became a team, a well-oiled machine, a customer-service-first empire. That year, we sold out the entire ship for the first time: more than twenty-four hundred Latin-music lovers, a mix of professional and nonprofessional dancers.

In 2015, we began to process all the booking and handle all the customer service in-house, rather than relying on third-party travel agencies. This helped us deliver much better customer service, increase efficiency and sales, grow as an independent company, and establish a foundation for even bigger things to come.

By 2015 and 2016, we were in a state of stratospheric joy: a cult of people who were so passionate about dancing, music, and this whole culture we love so much.

For 2017, we added a second cruise, making history by being the first-ever fully chartered Latin-dance cruise from the West Coast/Los Angeles and becoming the biggest Latin-dance-cruise company in the world.

And more—much more—remains to come.

I have a wonderful video from 2012 of a one-time artist, today a full-time employee of ADC and a dear friend, stating on camera that our dream was to someday have our own ship. At the time, it was something of a joke or a distant, silly dream. It didn't seem remotely possible.

But what I have learned in my career, my friends, is that when you get right down to it, anything is possible.

*Never, never, never give up.*

—Winston Churchill

The rest of this book is my little gift to my friends, my family, and the people who love ADC and the stories that go with it. I share more personal stories, but they are not just about me. Rather, the book is about the collection of tools that I used—mental, emotional, and physical—to pursue my dreams, whether it was moving to a new city and country, going to school, opening my first business, learning how to dance, or becoming the youngest person ever to charter a full ship for an event. In that way, this book itself is a guide, one that I hope you will find valuable, entertaining, and inspirational. It's my way of helping you kick-start your way to success and to finding your dreams and living them out! Dancing them out!

In dancing, it's all about having fun. So let's not just dance like no one is watching—let's dance like everyone is watching!

> *Twenty years from now you will be more disappointed by the things you didn't do than by the ones you did do. So throw off the bowlines. Sail away from the safe harbor. Catch the trade winds in your sails. Explore. Dream. Discover.*
>
> —Mark Twain

# The Basic Step

*The two most important days in your*
*life are the day you are born*
*and the day you find out why.*

—Mark Twain

In the art of dancing, the first step you ever learn is called the basic step. This step is the foundation. It's the surface upon which all other components of your dancing skill will be constructed: the rhythm, the timing, the interaction with your partner. Without the basic step, you don't have a foundation for professional dancing. To skip past this step and go into other parts of dancing would no doubt cause a great deal of confusion.

I've come to treasure this concept. Though it may sound simple, it's actually easy to overlook.

We're conditioned by so many forces, internal and external. We create expectations of ourselves. We react to other people's expectations of us. We're driven by material and immaterial impulses. Sometimes we go after something for egotistical reasons, while other times we're motivated to help other people. Often, our motives are overlapping and complex.

Accordingly, just as in the art of dance, the basic step can serve to clarify our actions in the dance of life itself.

In my eyes, the basic step is knowing each and every day what you want and why you want it. Once you identify these two things, you'll be operating on a firm foundation—a foundation that won't change quickly as a result of any random circumstance. And if it sounds easy, then just take a moment and examine your own situation: past, present, and future.

Do you always have clarity about what you want? From the time I was quite young, I knew I wanted to be a businessman, but I had no clue why I wanted this, much less what it entailed on any meaningful level.

Do you always have clarity about *why* you want what you want? In my case, I just had an image of myself. I guess I was in it for the money. My vision didn't go very deep. It felt right, which is certainly important, but I would have been hard pressed to explain to someone why I wanted to go into business.

If you asked ten different people if they wanted $1 billion, all of them would likely say yes. But if you went deeper, asking each of them the reason they wanted that $1 billion, the answers would differ in terms of depth and substance—and I'm even willing to bet that in some cases, there wouldn't be any answer at all.

It's amazing to me how many people have some sense of what they'd like to do professionally, yet lack a strong vision, drive, or purpose. When I've wondered exactly why that is, I could only conclude that vision, drive, and purpose cause fear. Moreover, these things require energy. It's easier to float here and there than to press forward with a concrete sense of what you desire.

I cannot emphasize enough how important it was for me to master this concept, master the basic step. In some cases, you might identify what you want, only to realize that the reasons you want it don't run deep enough for you. Once you recognize that, you might begin to see that you probably actually desire something else. Figuring out what that is may call for some reflection and self-examination, but once that process is complete, you're more likely not only to know what you want but also to be resolved and confident in your reasons for desiring it.

I remember reading a few books about how to franchise a business, a goal I had at the time. After I gained an understanding of what I needed to do well and how long it would take, I realized that I didn't want it anymore.

I simply didn't have a strong enough reason or purpose to go through what franchising would require. And I couldn't have been more grateful to learn that before it was too late.

Picture two guys who want to learn how to dance. Both of them know they want to dance, but neither one has ever thought about why. When pressed to do exactly that, one guy says he wants to get the glorious admiration and applause of audiences, meet some girls, and, um, that's about it. The other says he wants to cultivate his passion for music, gain a healthy new social hobby, and feel the gratification of knowing that he has mastered a new art.

In this example, I'm willing to bet that the guy who's in it for the glory or a date is less likely to stick to dancing over the long term than the guy who's in it for the mastery. When you choose what you want to do based on how other people will react to you, you're not really choosing to do an activity—instead, you're choosing a result, which is something that you can't always control.

There are many ways to get applause, and if this first dancer gets frustrated while learning to dance, he's likely to go out and pursue some other source of glory.

The second dancer, however, has a better shot at sustaining his interest, because he respects and longs for the art itself. In other words, the second dancer's *why* is stronger. Consequently—and this is the most important part—that dancer is more likely to hang in there and persist when the steps gets more complicated, when patience and practice are needed, and when times get hard.

*It takes twenty years to make an overnight success.*

—EDDIE CANTOR

We all inevitably face challenges. No matter how rosy a picture we might paint of ourselves for outsiders to see, it's guaranteed that we must deal with challenges, frustrations, questions, and confusion, at least on some level, some of the time. And since we know that challenges will come, it is critical that we operate with a strong basic step—a clear sense of purpose, backed up by solid motives.

For me, my basic step clicked in when I realized I didn't like working in the corporate world. I disliked the experience to such a degree that I was willing to go to extreme lengths to avoid it. I didn't want those emotions or that image of myself.

I didn't quite yet know what I did want, but knowing what I didn't want was a first step. (Pun intended!)

In a general sense, I felt that I wanted to be an entrepreneur. I also could see that dancing ignited my passion and that I wanted to touch people's lives somehow. When I put these realizations together, I was finally on my way. It was a good start for my deeper research on what I was searching for: my purpose, my real goal, my *why*. I can't even begin to tell you how many times the going got rough. I've lost count of the days when I wondered whether I was moving in the right direction— or even moving at all. But because I had established a strong basic step, I was able to keep on dancing until I turned the corner. It was easier for me to get motivated again, recharge, and keep on pushing. And today, although challenges still routinely arise, my personal *why* has hardened into steel.

We've talked about the *why* and of understanding the importance of knowing with clarity why you want to achieve your goals. But I'd like to briefly add to this concept some comments about the importance of having fun.

To have fun, do something you *love.*

When you do something you enjoy and it's effortless and easy, you will want to keep on doing it more. In other words, it won't feel like work to you.

And that feeling that your work isn't like work is one of the great keys to success.

There's a myth out there that you have to drive yourself into the ground to be successful, because the harder you work, the more results you get. There's some measure of truth to this, but when true passion fuels the work and you're having fun, in my opinion, you'll work that much harder.

Not only that, it will feel kind of like intense play.

When you talk to dancers, they'll always tell you that above all else, their art is always about having fun. Sure, you have to think about the timing and the steps and the next move you need to execute and so on, but beyond all that, you still want to have fun.

With that in mind, one of the first steps to being successful is just finding something you like to do.

After all, look at some of the most successful people in the world. Nobody has to bend Michael Jordan's arm and convince him to play basketball; he just loves to play. Nobody has to put a megaphone up to Steven Spielberg's ear and insist that he make movies; he just loves to tell stories on film. Nobody has to put on a cheerleader's costume and cheer Beyoncé on before she goes onstage; she just loves to sing and perform.

The same goes for dancers.

Sure, the path is not always easy. You have to practice. You may get hurt. You'll have setbacks. Maybe you won't make money. But still, if that enjoyment of the process is there, it will carry you an amazing distance. All the traffic, the injuries, the stress, and the so-called "failures" will be worth it when you reach that joy of getting your dance routine down just right.

So much of my own journey was driven by the desire to have fun. It's actually funny to think that I used to be this kid who just wanted to have fun. And now I've built my business around the concept of having fun. Even though I did a lot of growing and maturing in between, becoming more serious on many levels, I've never let go of that will to simply enjoy myself.

For starters, I liked the whole idea of having my own business. I also liked music, and I really liked dancing. So—voila! My own dance studio! But of course, it went even further than that. I love few things more than taking vacations. And I really, really love the ocean.

So look at what we have here: a dance cruise!

The path was far from direct, but at every step along the way, the journey was fueled, at its roots, by the desire to have fun.

The question then becomes, what makes you want to jump out of bed in the morning? What fills you with so much passion that you can't stop thinking about it and wouldn't dream of only doing it halfway?

Whatever your particular answer is, it's probably your calling. Stay open minded, look for opportunities, develop the habit of converting negatives into positives, and don't take no for an answer.

This doesn't mean the world will agree—at least not right away. There will be hard days. For me, there are still plenty of hard days! But I'll tell you something: the hard days are far fewer than the pleasant days, because I have stuck to doing something that makes me want to leap out of bed in the morning, keeps me awake at night, and propels me even when I'm tired. It's no surprise that I barely get any sleep for the four days of an ADC cruise.

Where do I find that energy? Now you know.

However, if you dread getting out of bed each morning and can't stand going to the job you already have, then it's probably time for a change. You're out of alignment with your calling. Let somebody else do that job! I'm sure that plenty of people would be thrilled to have it. As for you, you're better off doing something that makes your heart sing.

I've loved the following piece of advice ever since I first heard it: if you're looking for a book and you can't find it, write it. This advice can be modified to inspire entrepreneurship: if you're looking for a business or service and you can't find it, provide it.

Your search for that thing is really an *idea* in disguise, and it's an idea you probably need to follow through on.

# Fast-Tempo Version

- **Master the *basic step*—know what you want and why you want it**
- **Do something that you love, always!**

# FOCUS ON YOUR DANCE PARTNER

*Aim for service and success will follow.*

—ALBERT SCHWEITZER

Walk into any social event, dance party, or club, and you can easily spot a dancer trying to get your attention. He will normally try to execute some fancy, flashy move, regardless of his or his partner's level of skill. He'll scream, stomp the floor, or simply try to show off his ridiculous new hat, jacket, suit, or any other random accessory that even Lady Gaga wouldn't wear.

While discussing the basic step, we have covered territory relating to self-examination. Ironically, though, once you're out there on the floor, dancing with a secure sense of purpose as your foundation, it is absolutely critical to focus on your partner.

This may sound counterintuitive. Indeed, it's a little scary at first: you're relinquishing some attention for the sake of directing attention to someone else. But I assure you that in business, relationships, and almost everywhere else, the more you set your focus outward, away from yourself and onto others, the greater you will succeed.

It's so common to see beginning dancers out on the dance floor, looking around, conscious of who's looking at them, who's beside them, and whom they should dance with next. They're worried about who's looking because they're eager to make a good impression or simply show off. They're worried about who's nearby because they're concerned about staying ahead of the competition. And instead of being in the moment, focusing on the dance and having fun, they're worrying about whom they should dance with next.

Fellas, I cannot even begin to tell you how many times I've heard ladies complain about this. They simply hate inattentive dance partners. They want you to connect with them not only as their partner but also as their leader for the course of a three- to four-minute song, which isn't really asking a lot. In dancing, it's often said that the lady is the picture, and the guy is the frame. Know what I mean? The guy is there to help make the lady look good. So why not focus on your dance partner? Dance at her level, regardless of yours, and make her look good. In doing so, you'll be making yourself look good.

Sure, it's natural to want to look good and keep up with (and outdo) the competition and to know what is going to happen next. I would never recommend that somebody not be aware of all these things. However, first and foremost, when you're out there dancing, *focus on and dance with your partner!*

You want people to say you dance well? Focus on your dance partner.

You want a line of people waiting to dance with you? Focus on your dance partner.

You want to have fun? Focus...

You know the rest.

Everywhere we go, we see that the person who worries about him- or herself at the expense of everybody else creates problems.

But we're all together on the same dance floor, dancing to the same music, and we therefore are designed to cooperate with and help one another. By directing all our focus inward, toward our own pressing concerns, we miss the chance to be of value to others. And only when we are of value can we be loved and therefore have a chance at succeeding.

The other important aspect of focusing on our dance partners is that it's simply more *fun*. We can feel free to take the burden off of ourselves. We can allow our bodies to do what they will, in proportion to how much experience and talent we each have. What a relief to let ourselves go!

We don't have to worry about not being taken care of, because when we focus on our dance partners, our partners in turn focus on us. So we're covered; our dance partners have our backs. With this in mind, we can actually cut loose, make things happen, and accumulate energy, keeping the show going with maximum love and joy.

Business isn't always fun; instead, it's often challenging. But in business, I work every day to keep all avenues fun, open, and clear. In that context, my dance partners are my customers and the people with whom I work. It's about our clients and about the greater good of our company. It's never all about an individual, or anything else for that matter.

*Do what you do so well that they will want*
*to see it again and bring their friends.*

—WALT DISNEY

When it comes to my customers, I'm sensitive. After starting my dance studio, I always marveled when a new student came in for the first time. I consistently reminded my staff that this student not only had to spend his or her hard-earned dollars but also had to pick up the phone, orchestrate his or her schedule, get in the car and drive over to us, find parking, bring the right clothes and shoes, and give him- or herself over to the class for its duration.

These new students were trying something new, in front of other people, while getting out of their comfort zones. It was not only demanding—it was *scary*.

All of that is *huge!*

I'm not just talking about the entire process. I think every step of it is enormous. I remember the first time I took dance lessons in Miami. Picking up that phone was a major step. Not only was I looking for fun and excitement but I was also seeking to expand my social life. It meant something to me. It wasn't just some mindless phone call.

The dance cruises we produce are no exception. As we're known to say over and over again, "We take your vacation very seriously." It sounds a bit playful, but it happens to be true. Amid all of their vacation options, our clients decided to choose our product. That puts the burden on us to deliver as magnificent, exciting, and transforming an experience as humanly possible.

My employees are my dance partners as well. The key to my individual success is identifying and utilizing their talents, motivating them, acknowledging and appreciating them, and—above all—making sure we all have fun during the process. My job isn't to boss them around; instead, it's to liberate their talents and skills so that all of us can push the enterprise forward.

Often, people close to me try to turn my attention to what those planning other events are doing: what talent they book, what venues that they choose, and so forth. Now, this kind of thing is extremely important if your business is devoted to one-and-done kinds of events, but if you are here for the long run, your main focus should be on your customers' needs and the addition of value to your own product—not that of others. So avoid the common mistake of thinking your competition is your dance partner. Don't put too much focus on him or her. This doesn't mean your competitors are your enemies. Not at all. It simply means that they're not what's important. Let them do what they do, at whatever level they like. It's not worth obsessing over their activities. At most, give them, say, 20 percent of your attention, and save the rest for your dance partner. There's no easier way to get lost in business than to be caught up in playing games with one's competitors. Imagine a marathon runner who's out there looking at everyone ahead of and behind him rather than focusing on his own performance. That's when all the will and substance go out of him!

Focusing on the competition is a waste of energy. You become too urgent, too eager to win. In the meantime, who loses?

That's right: your customers and your team.

Your dance partners.

⌒

I once went for a walk with an artist I work with, and we started discussing how many events were trying to be like ADC. These were not necessarily aboard a cruise, but they were dance events that promoted workshops, shows, and an all-around great time. However, in many cases, the producers of these events don't seem to care about the services they're providing and promoting.

Funnily enough, these same promoters who don't put a lot of love into the service they provide complain about the Latin-dance industry. "There's no money in dancing," they'll say. "You can't make a dime in this industry," they'll declare. "This community/ city doesn't support it," they'll claim.

Sure, I can see where they're coming from. It's not like Latin dance is a luxury industry on par with yoga or spas. But I'm over here remembering all the events I've attended where the producers just didn't deliver.

They promise you a world-class show. They promise you this; they promise you that. Top notch. State of the art. Everything under the sun. And then, after they fail to deliver, they go on complaining about how there's no money in dancing!

Forget about delivering. Instead, focus your aim higher. What about overdelivering?

What about bonus items? And little surprises?

The point is that when you treat your dance partner like a queen—or a king—you'll get to dance like royalty, despite the supposed limits of whatever industry you find yourself in. Don't underestimate your clients. They are smart, just like you—if not more so! "If you build it, they will come," they say.

In other words, if you add value and deliver something worth their time and money, they will be there, and they will bring their friends!

# Fast-Tempo Version

- *Focus on your dance partner.* It's not about you; rather, it's about those around you.
- Don't waste time focusing on your competitors. Instead, focus on your customers, your product, and your team.
- Treat your dance partners like queens (and kings)!

# COMMIT TO THE DANCE

*Discipline is the bridge between goals and accomplishment.*

—JIM ROHN

Let's dance!

Once you know what you want and why you want it, it's time to take things to the next level by making a commitment, being certain, and having conviction. Commitment for me isn't a light thing. It's *everything*. Commitment is actually a contract between you and whatever you're committing to. You're saying, in other words, you're *in it* now and there's no turning back.

When people commit, they commit 100 percent. Somebody who's 99 percent committed isn't truly committed at all. The energy, mind-set, and attitude of being in that partial state of commitment are unbearable. The key is not to have one foot dangling out the door. The words *all in* have actual meaning behind them. Either you're in or you're out. There's no in between.

A guy who cheats on his wife once in a while but controls himself most of the time isn't "mostly" committed. He's left the marriage. His body may still be present in the same home as his wife, but the rest of him is away somewhere.

And I don't know about you, but I don't like the feeling of being in two worlds at once. When you're not committed, your mind wanders. You dabble. You think you might want to try out this or that instead. Your sense of purpose is cloudy. People don't quite grasp what your specialty is or where you might be headed.

But when you're committed, you're in a single world. It's not only about being focused but also about consciously choosing to have a relationship with that focus. You're determined to be focused on $x$, $y$, or $z$ for as long as doing so serves you.

That's commitment.

And it's awesome.

# USING CONFIDENT LANGUAGE

So much of being committed simply boils down to your attitude. One thing that's worked for me over the years has been paying attention to the words I use to express myself. Language is a critical tool we all use. Words aren't just little sounds we make. They're charged with meaning and actual energy.

Have you ever been around someone who constantly uses negative words and—worse yet—uses words that aren't backed up by any confidence? It feels horrible, doesn't it? The language just sort of dribbles off that person's tongue, failing at every turn to make you feel inspired or remotely happy.

When I'm around people like that, I promptly seek out a wall to bang my head against.

Confident language is so important. In fact, I'm going to say that if you can't express yourself with confidence, then you probably aren't able to make a true commitment. What sounds better to you, someone who hopes to be successful or someone who knows he will be successful?

Picture a single guy who really wants a girlfriend. His choice of language in talking about this is "I hope someday I'll have a girlfriend."

Well, this isn't really a horse worth betting on, is it? I mean, I'm not about to go to the bank and withdraw all my money so I can wager that this guy's going to have a girlfriend anytime soon.

But then there's another guy. He, too, is single, but he talks about it differently. He doesn't say, "I hope." No, this guy's committed to his search. He says, "I know someday I'll have a girlfriend."

Huge difference. I mean, granted, it's not worth betting all your money on, but if you had the choice between betting on one or the other, which one would you choose?

And, please, don't tell me the guy who says "hope" is more realistic. Sure, no one knows with certainty what the future holds. (Except for psychics, of course, but that's a whole other story...) And there is a chance that Mr. Hope will get a girlfriend before Mr. Know does. But you know what? I'm still banking on Mr. Know. Because that guy's got confidence in his blood. That guy's a true believer in his own potential and the destiny that awaits him.

⌒

Back when I started my dance studio, I had an insight about the way I use language. Every time I said something like "I'm going to work" or "I'm going to my job," I just kind of got this gray, heavy feeling. There's almost a universal tone that kicks in when people say they're going to work. Their shoulders sag. They let out a sigh. It's not the sort of thing that people tend to declare with gusto, pumping their fists and smiling from ear to ear.

I didn't like that feeling, so I decided to change all that.

My tone didn't change; instead, my language changed. I didn't say I was going to "work" or to my "job," but rather that I was going to my "studio." I actually told the staff to start engaging in the same word choices. Sure, on a technical level, it was our job, but the word "studio" raised the discussion to a higher level. A studio is a creative space. A studio is a place of class. The word "studio" doesn't bring to mind labor or paychecks or hours on the clock. It brings to mind creativity, elegance, and, most importantly, our ultimate passion—dancing!

This subtle shift turned out to be not so subtle after all. In fact, it was extremely powerful. I was rewiring our studio's culture. As we all know, different cultures have different languages. Often, one culture has a word for something that another culture does not. I firmly believe that these subtle yet powerful distinctions create human beings' vastly different attitudes.

So at my studio—in my little culture—words like "job" or "work" came to be viewed as negatives. They were spirit killers. They were the types of things that other people had to worry about—not us. That's one of the main reasons we all came together and danced: to leave all that behind.

Negativity is not allowed here.

And as we cast such words aside, our attitude about what we were doing improved, and our commitment to doing it followed.

Take a long look at the words you're using. Do you call your spouse a "ball and chain"? Do you call your car or cell phone a "piece of trash"? What kinds of attitudes are you communicating through your personal use of language? Chances are, if you're describing yourself and the things you have, as well as the people you know, in negative or low-confidence terms, then you're probably not experiencing much in the way of commitment.

But by turning your language and your attitude around, you can find true commitment, without a doubt. Doing this will unconsciously raise your energy and your actual spirit, and you will then see improvements in everything that you do.

*Having bad grammar is like wearing torn clothes.*

—LISA JEFFERY

In general (hopefully), we try to cultivate good habits. We put thought and care into things like how we dress, what shape we keep our bodies in, and how we behave in relation to where we are and what we're up to. But how much thought do we put into our own words? Maybe we sometimes hold back from cursing or try to use bigger words if we're talking to someone smart—but it's so wise to gravitate toward positive words. Just like when we look good and have good manners, when we use positive language it only stands to up our voltage as human beings.

For me, realizing this was a breakthrough, and I've paid close attention to it ever since.

# BURN YOUR SHIP

I know, I know—why is a guy who runs cruise ships subtitling this section "Burn Your Ship"?

Well, for me, the "burn your ship" concept is absolutely critical when it comes to committing to anything whatsoever. I am thrilled to share this idea with you because over time, I've learned when facing different situations to think about whatever's holding me back, and then—*bam*—I can eliminate it and get back to moving forward.

35

This concept comes from an old war story. A general's army arrived on a new shore, intent upon invading. The army was ready to advance, but before they had a chance to do so, the general issued a surprising order. "Turn back around, go to the ships, and burn them!" he commanded.

Needless to say, his men couldn't believe their ears. "Um, general…" one man stepped forward and said.

"Yes?" the general replied.

"You do realize that the ships are the things we came here on…"

"Sure."

"And, um…you do realize that the ships are the things we need to get back home…"

"Nope!"

"How come?"

"Because this *is* home, son! Now get to work!"

It wasn't the most natural or intuitive process in the world, but, hey, an order was an order, so those troops had to do as they were told. Before they did what they had gone there for, which was to stage an invasion, they gathered some wood, got a fire going, dipped the wood into the fire, and hurled the burning pieces of wood at the very ships they had sailed in on.

I'm sure it was quite a sight to see, with all those ships spewing fire up into the air. It was probably an incredible sight not only for the invading army but also for anybody in the opposing army who caught what was going on.

"These guys must be crazy!" they probably yelled.

Or clueless.

But was the general who gave the order crazy or clueless? Well, maybe! When you think about it, though, his strategy was pretty sane and wise. He was creating an environment in which failure was not an option. He knew that in battle, you can win, you can lose, or you can run away. Once you delete "run away" from the list of options, you become that much more determined to win. Nothing motivates like discomfort. Comfort, however, has a way of making people go soft.

That general knew that if his army recognized there was no possible way of getting home, they would be determined to fight that much harder.

Does that sound irrational? Amazing? Wild?

Good!

That's the case because we are about to discuss how important it is to find your "ship" and burn it! That, my friends, is the true meaning of commitment. Commitment is not just a mental process. Commitment is not just about switching out low-confidence words for high-confidence ones. No, commitment actually calls for more drastic measures, such as choosing to erase any escape routes for yourself.

When I moved to Los Angeles, I loved the new culture and lifestyle the city offered. It's a town filled with dreamers. People have come here from all over the world to pursue the dreams in their hearts. And for every dreamer out here, I can guarantee you there was somebody in his or her life who advised him or her to have a Plan B—"something to fall back on," just in case the dream didn't work out.

But the general who told his soldiers to burn their ships wasn't dealing in any fallback measures. Hell no. As far as that guy was concerned, it was Plan A or nothing.

Period.

My own path has been filled with "burn your ship" moments.

Feel free to call me a reckless lunatic, but the truth is that by not having a ship to climb back onto, I've essentially forced myself into choosing between a state of success or no success. My commitments have at times been overwhelming, even scary, but you know what's worse than being overwhelmed and scared? Not even trying. Selling out. Taking a Plan B. Doing something that doesn't ignite your passions, much less your soul.

When you do what you want, you won't regret it even if you fail, because at one point, it was indeed exactly what you wanted. And if you don't do it, you will just live with the nagging question: what if?

That, to me, is way worse than being afraid.

*The best way to predict your future is to create it.*

—PETER DUCKER

When I was younger and I moved to Miami, I left my car back at home. For me, this car was my entire world. It was my freedom. It was my independence. But as I got settled in Miami, I called my dad and told him to sell the car. Why? Because I realized that if it wasn't waiting for me at home, I'd really having nothing calling me back there. Sure, I had my family, whom I love very much, but they weren't the people I was intent upon spending time with. And because I was so young, my car represented a big, bright symbol of my old way of life: hanging out with friends, having fun, and getting into adventures. But I was committed to having a whole new kind of adventure in Miami. Accordingly, I burned my ship. There would be no exit door for me from that scenario.

Later, I started losing weight. Over the course of three years, I took off about forty pounds. During that experience, my "burn your ship" moment was to give away all my large-size clothes to Goodwill when they no longer fit. Why? If I had those clothes around, I might have been tempted to fill them up again—know what I mean? But with only smaller clothes in the house, I had no choice but to hang on to my newly small body. And no way would I allow myself to buy larger clothes again, not after I'd burned my ship.

When I made the move from Miami to Los Angeles, I had the option of leaving some of my stuff in storage back in Miami. But I chose not to. I didn't want any physical tie to Miami. Now, sure, I can go back to Miami anytime I want, but, psychologically, the difference between having belongings there and having nothing there was huge to me. It was a part of my process to commit to LA and the goals I had there. So I chose to wipe that slate clean. To cut all ties. To commit to my new future, in other words. I burned my ship.

Last but not least is the example of ADC.

When I knew that this was what I wanted to do, that it's where my passion lies and what makes me happy—and when I also had a financial plan that would satisfy my financial growth goals—it was time to burn my ships again and go all in.

That time, it was my dance studio, my creation, my baby, which had taken me so much work to get going before it finally became a business that supported me financially and spiritually. Regardless, I just knew I couldn't do both. If I really wanted to leave the safe shore and give ADC the best chance possible at being as good as I could make it, then I'd have to give it more time, travel more...go *all in*.

So I did it.

It wasn't easy or fast. I had to try my best to find someone who would take care of the studio. By then, it wasn't just a business. The employees had become my extended family, and the students had as well. So I had to make sure I could leave it in good hands.

I tried my best, but I also had a deadline. Though I pushed things a bit longer than I had planned, eventually, gradually, I took a step back and turned it over.

For me, without question, my future was Aventura Dance Cruise.

And so, a new chapter in my life began. There was no way back. It was time to make it happen.

Time to make *ship* happen!

⌒

So much of the time, when I talk to a friend who is moving, I find out that he or she is leaving some stuff at the place he or she is allegedly moving out of. Maybe it's that person's parents' house. Maybe it's an apartment the person shared with a roommate, but now he or she is going to try out living with a girlfriend or boyfriend. To my mind, leaving some stuff behind is the ultimate psychological symbol of having no real and full commitment. You're essentially leaving a trail between your new environment and your old one. It's all too easy to go back to your childhood bedroom when it's still decorated with all your stuff, right? But what if that room's been stripped clean and become anonymous? Whole different story, then. You'd feel a little strange about going back there, and you'd certainly be more aware of the transition.

I recall a friend of mine who declared that, after years as a smoker, she was finally done with smoking. But one day, I noticed something funny in her house: a new pack of cigarettes! I dangled it in front of her, asking her WTF was going on. She said she had received them as a gift a long time ago, from a friend who had bought them at the duty-free shop at the airport. She'd kept them "just in case." She didn't want to throw them out, as that would be a "waste." But for me, "just in case" is the ultimate signal of noncommitment! I told her to throw those cigarettes away, because they were just an easy pathway back to smoking—a ship prepared to carry her back home.

So she tossed them out and has never again revisited her habit. That was her "burn your ship" moment, and I couldn't be more proud of her.

My own most recent "burn your ship" moment came when I decided to sell my dance studio. It was time to focus purely on the cruise company. Granted, the cruises were bringing in more income than the studio, but for years, the studio had been my bread and butter. I'd put food on my table through that studio. Cutting that cord was not so easy. But I had to cut it, as I was committed to my new adventure.

What I have found really fascinating is that if you don't cut that cord, it just keeps growing bigger. Having your ship sitting there at the shoreline isn't something that just lingers at the back of your mind. It can actually blossom into a full-blown obsession! Think about it. Consider my friend's pack of cigarettes, just sitting there, waiting to be smoked. The more days she went without smoking, the more of an option I'm sure that pack came to be. It's like keeping your ex's phone number in your phone's contact list. Inevitably, some days are challenging. Some days, you just want to retreat back into your safety zone.

But if there's no safety zone awaiting you, then you have no choice but to keep pressing forward—through the challenges, through the uncertainty, into the newness, and toward your dreams.

And that, my friends, is commitment without compromise.

# Failure Can Start, But Only Success Can Finish

No matter what I've done, there have always been people who let me know I didn't stand a chance. They were the "realistic" ones—also known as the "negative" ones.

It's been pretty amazing, actually. As it turns out, you can find these people absolutely anywhere on earth, no matter *what* you're trying to do!

When I opened my dance studio, these people told me that 80 percent of small businesses close within the first year.

When I started to study and play the stock market, these people told me that 95 percent of people lose money in the stock market.

Later, they told me that most dance events lose money. They also let me know that the economy was so bad that nobody stood a chance!

"You can't get a full ship if you don't have money," they said.

"You need to have money to make money," they said.

Time and time again, I just nodded and tried to stay as humble as possible, while this little voice inside of me would whisper, "Watch this…"

My small business didn't close in the first year. We made it to the fifth and beyond. I made money playing stocks. I earned my living through dance events. The bad economy did not destroy me. In fact, I actually got established during it. I was able to get a full-ship charter through bookings, without paying out up-front cash, because I managed to earn the trust, sympathy, and friendship of the cruise line's top executives. I didn't need to have money to make money.

As all these things worked out, one after the other, I naturally was a little curious as to how they'd occurred, despite all these people saying it wasn't possible. I was proud of myself, but I knew that I wasn't some odds-defying mythical creature.

So what was going on, exactly?

*Fall seven times, stand up eight.*

—JAPANESE PROVERB

In short, I just stuck with everything I tried. I failed a lot, over and over again. I had many bleak and challenging days. But I kept on going, kept on pushing.

The reason I succeeded, I believe, is simply because I was persistent. "No" was one word I never learned in school.

Starting something is easy. Staying with it is hard. To be consistent, to keep on believing, to not fold and simply give up is what takes real grit. That's exactly where most people fail for good.

The successful people are the ones who not only start but also finish.

The successful people are the ones who know the odds may be against most people—but are not necessarily against them.

Most people do not stick it out. Most people go home. Most people settle.

If you want to be successful, settling should *never* be an option.

# FAST-TEMPO VERSION

- **Commit to what you're doing 100 percent. (At least!)**
- **Use confident and positive language; it will push you.**
- *Burn your ship*—**don't leave yourself with any easy ways out.**
- **Finish what you started—that's what counts!**

# HIT THE DANCE FLOOR

*To avoid criticism, do nothing, say nothing, and be nothing.*

—ELBERT HUBBARD

Here we go again—another song: let's dance!

It's time to take action. This is the part when you grab your partner and tear it up on the dance floor. However, taking action isn't only about going out there and doing things. More importantly, it's about developing and promoting a habit of taking risks. Try new moves, dare, take chances, and see what the dance will bring and how it will develop.

*Limits, like fears, are often just an illusion.*

—MICHAEL JORDAN

It's normal to be afraid to take a risk. We don't want our daily routines and patterns to be interrupted by anything unexpected. But here is the real risk: if you don't take any risk, nothing amazing will ever happen. Sure, you might get lucky here or there, falling into some exciting circumstances, but without a habit of taking risks, you'll never find yourself living day-to-day in an exciting/excited fashion.

The cool thing about taking risks is that once you do it a couple of times, it becomes far less threatening and menacing to you. It doesn't even matter what the risks are. They can be big, small, or medium—but once you're used to dealing with risk, you generally have the confidence to keep on heading into risky situations. We have to break the rules—not the law— but we have to break the rules if we want to achieve something great. Otherwise, where is the fun, thrill, or excitement in life?

Mind you, the point of taking risks isn't just to be daring. It's not to prove how wild or reckless you can be. Though people can get some pride out of being wild, the point I'm making here is that there can be no meaningful action without risk. Think about it: What does action without risk look like? Can a sports team score without lessening its defense? Can a boxer punch without uncovering his face? Can a boat explore new oceans without leaving the safety of the shore?

Action without risk is humdrum. It's banal. Routine. Worst of all, it's safe. For the actions you take from day-to-day to have any impact whatsoever on your future, they have to take you out of your comfort zone.

When you're investing in the stock market, financial advisers teach you that, depending on where you are in life and what your financial goals are, you should have some of your money in safe stocks, some in medium-risk stocks, and a small percentage in high-risk stocks. Why? Because you never know—you might get lucky. But also, this approach is good for the mind. It keeps you excited and "in the game." It's healthy for you. You need that risk. Without it, you might get bored and make much worse moves. We simply need that excitement, for the soul and to have fun!

# Embracing Discomfort

*I don't look to jump over seven-foot bars: I look
around for one-foot bars that I can step over.*

—Warren Buffett

Now, once you're taking meaningful action, which means taking risks—which means being outside of your comfort zone—you don't necessarily have to exist in a moment-to-moment state of discomfort. Risk doesn't have to be overwhelming and terrifying to count as risk. No, I'm not here to encourage discomfort. (Even though good is the enemy of great!)

Instead, you should know how to manage your discomfort.

So how do you do that? Simple: you break your large tasks down into small tasks. To shift from dancing to basketball for just a moment, I remember when Kobe Bryant announced his retirement. People were congratulating him and asking him about his long career. He credited Phil Jackson, his longtime coach, with teaching him how to break down big things into smaller units, like years into months, seasons into games, games into quarters, so he could focus on getting through them just one challenge at a time, especially when it came to dealing with recovering from injuries and fatigue from his long career.

This practice is effective whether you're talking about time or any other unit of measurement. When you eat a meal, you don't just pour it all down your throat (however tempting that may be at times); instead, you break it down into bites. When you cross the street, you don't go galloping with great long strides; rather, you simply take it one step at a time. These are common examples, but isn't it funny to see how often we forget to break things down into manageable units? That's especially true of tasks that challenge us. We have a tendency to walk around catching our breath because we can't get over how challenging a given task is. But the mistake we're making is not seeing the task as a series of smaller, more manageable steps.

Take what we do at ADC as an example. We produce theme cruises with more than twenty-four hundred people aboard each one, entertain them nonstop for between seventy-two and ninety-six hours, take them overseas, and oversee their individual vacation needs, all while managing a steep financial risk, for heaven's sake! When you put it that way, our responsibilities sound completely overwhelming.

The way I get through it is by taking it piece by piece. Each unit has its own compartment. Marketing is one thing. Planning is another. Budgeting is another. Customer service is yet another. The logistics of being at sea has its own compartment, and so does choosing the talent, the food, the music, and so on. It's the same with creating our intensely busy event schedule: we approach it one day at a time, one hour at a time, one event at a time.

It all comes down to bite-size pieces. Not only do they save you from choking on your food but also they allow you to savor the meal.

Fun Fact: each year has 365 days in it. So if you want to make $1 million a year, you have to make approximately $2,740 each day. It sounds a bit more realistic and achievable when you think about it this way, no?

# THE POWER OF SMALL ACCOMPLISHMENTS: IT ALL ADDS UP

Take the basic step, add a cross-body lead, add a right turn, and then—why not?—also add a left turn, thrown in some styling, take a few basic steps to catch your breath, mix and match everything again as you wish, and what do you get?

You are dancing!

We often overlook the small steps we take as well as the so-called "small" accomplishments. But small accomplishments are so important because they are in fact steppingstones to larger accomplishments.

Focus on your own journey, your own accomplishments, and you will see a beautiful thing happen: the more little things you achieve, the more confident you become about achieving large things. It takes time. It takes patience. It will inevitably involve some setbacks and failures. But as you attain some smaller goals, you'll find yourself more naturally and confidently dreaming up larger ones.

Dance to enough songs, attend enough dance events, and before you know it, when a fast song or a supposedly "hard" dance comes up, maybe a great dancer whom you once were intimidated to dance with will be there right alongside you.

You've got this.

At the dance studio, once we got started, I wanted to sign up one new member per week. Once I saw that that was possible, I kicked the number up a notch. Before I knew it, my weekly membership goal was twenty, then thirty, and on and on.

In 1954, Roger Bannister broke the four-minute barrier for the mile run. No one had ever done that before, and it had long seemed almost impossible. Then, barely a year after he smashed the record, someone else ran a mile in under four minutes. Some more runners did it after that. Now it's almost routine. Even strong high schoolers have been known to run four-minute miles.

Once Bannister crashed through that barrier, the rest of the world saw it was possible, and the previous record, which had stood for nine years, was broken routinely.

So back to my dance studio, maybe one new member a week sounds like an easy goal. But for me, with respect to trying something new, it was huge. Once I conquered that milestone and saw what was possible, I took more ambitious actions and pulled off more ambitious goals.

Don't wish it were easier; instead, wish you were stronger.

Don't ask for it to be simpler; rather, become smarter.

That's the way to make things happen and, of course, to make *ship* happen...

## Making Ship Happen

"Making ship happen" has become something of a company motto here at ADC. In addition to all our other values, the idea of "making ship happen" is absolutely critical. It's all about pushing things forward, no matter what, no excuses. It's about staying determined, keeping your energy high, and doing whatever must be done to narrow the distance between yourself and your goal. After all, it's the doers who actually get things accomplished. Success isn't about where you are in life but rather how willing you are to go for it and make ship happen.

When my company first started out, we always had to work with the cruise line through a travel agency. In other words, even though we essentially *were* the cruise, the travel agency was the provider on paper. Meanwhile, I was the one who knew all the details about what it took to make ADC happen. So I always found myself funneling information through the travel agency to the cruise line, and as you can imagine, things regularly got lost in translation. Sure, the people at the travel agency were nice and everything, but—let's face it—once they got their money, they were perhaps slightly less interested in attending to the little details than I was.

I'll never forget our 2011 cruise. We had an ice-skating rink on the ship, decked out with a full theater setup. Throughout the ice-skating event, I was regularly going onstage and acting as the host, wearing an enormous smile on my face. But backstage, it was a different story...

Backstage, I had a representative from the cruise line telling me that a party we'd scheduled for *an hour later* was nowhere on their books! Can you imagine what would happen if seven hundred people who were promised a party did not get their party? Try and tell a dancer he or she can't dance—good luck! A full-blown riot would probably be the least of it.

I told the woman from the cruise company to call the office and get approval. But the problem was, everybody from the office was fast asleep and off for the weekend.

It was a Saturday night, and there we were, in the middle of the ocean, trying to conjure up a party out of thin air.

The funny part was that, more than at any other time in my career, I had to switch back and forth between my negotiating hat and my hosting hat at amazing speeds. I'd be backstage, unsmiling, telling the cruise line woman that something had to be done to solve this right away, and then I'd be called back up to the microphone, where I'd smile and laugh and introduce the next act. Then—*boom*—I'd lose the smile, go backstage, and continue giving the cruise line rep a piece of my mind.

Looking back, it's something I laugh about now. At the time, though, I was determined to keep the show going no matter what.

And that's exactly what I mean by "making ship happen."

In 2012, these kinds of issues continued. The travel agency made promises, only for them to be broken by the cruise line. Finally, I'd had enough of this situation and I took the situation in hand. I respected the cruise line's policy of not communicating with me since I technically was not the client, but at a certain point, that policy had to bend. I asked, "I'm bringing more than one thousand people aboard your ship, and you can't even talk to me?"

If I had been running that cruise line, I would not have kept that policy in place in such a situation. So I did something about it. I made ship happen. I got online and started searching for e-mail addresses. Anybody who had an e-mail address with that specific cruise line's name in it was going to hear from me. I didn't care if it was a receptionist, a window washer, a board director, an owner, or you name it. I was determined to make some serious contact. I also called everyone, sent old-school postal mail, sent online customer-service messages, whatever.

Was it noisy? Yes. Was it over the line? Of course.

Did it work? You better believe it!

The thing about being noisy is that, although people may not like you for it at first, they'll usually respect you for what you did later, presuming you have an objective that's within reason. Nowadays, since ADC has moved into doing full-ship charters, the people at the cruise line office treat me with a lot of respect, just as I greatly respect them. I'm not that problematic kid whom they want to keep quiet anymore. Now I'm their partner, and they're looking to grow with me.

⌒

That doesn't mean I don't still make ship happen. On some level, I'll always be that hungry kid who built up ADC from the ground (or the ocean) floor.

I remember one time when a transportation company I gave lots of business to was nice enough to rent a limousine for my assistant and me. It was a wonderful gesture, but little did they know how much equipment I traveled with to make ADC happen. I mean, cables, speakers, mixers, banners...everything it takes to pull off a cruise event. So it was hilarious to see the look on the limo driver's face when I started cramming all that stuff into the vehicle. And it was even funnier when we pulled up to the port and people started looking at us: "Wow! Who are these fancy people showing up?" And then we stepped outside and started dragging along more gear than a rock band.

Before I had access to the limo, I used to rent a big car and lug everything all by myself. People still joke with me about how I carried everything alone. A couple of girls worked for me, but they weren't going to carry speakers and cables—besides, they worked hard enough as it was. Besides, back in the day, I had been a deejay, so I was used to carting equipment back and forth.

The craziest part was that the cruise line didn't give me any storage space aboard the ship, as they didn't want the liability. Gotta love those cruise line policies! They wouldn't even loan me a dolly so I could roll the stuff back and forth. So not only was I the maniac carrying all this stuff with me but I was also stuffing it all inside my own cabin. If you've ever seen the interior of a cruise-ship cabin, you know how tiny those places can be. How I managed to sleep in there remains a mystery.

That's not to say I really had much time for sleeping, though. Those cruises were often an exciting, wild blur to me. In the early days, for five straight cruises, I was always on my feet, rushing speakers from my cabin, struggling up and down flights of steps, waiting forever to catch those elevators, building party setups, and then—*boom*—dancing and, after that, breaking everything down at four or five in the morning and getting it all back to my room for the following day. A lot of the time, the deejay would be exhausted and just crash, which meant I was alone to handle the equipment. It wasn't unusual for me to fall asleep at the crack of dawn and then wake up at 7:00 a.m. so I could make my way to the dance workshops.

Speaking of exhaustion, I remember one year when we organized a sunset beach party, and I learned a major lesson about not putting on shows after beach parties. See, we threw this really wild beach party. Everyone was dancing out on the sand. People were pouring drinks down their throats. And before we knew it, the sun was setting. We were ecstatic. It was wondrous. Beautiful.

Then it started to rain.

I instantly ducked for cover. As fast as my feet would carry me, I ran for shelter. But when I looked up and turned around, I realized that I'd run away all alone! My guests were still out there on the sand, dancing in the rain. What a glorious sight! I love our people! I ran back out there and joined them. The chaos, the energy, the spontaneity of it—that event was a classic.

As you might have guessed, a lot of people got pretty tipsy out there. Gradually, they stumbled back toward the ship. Some of them were ADC staff members, and in fact, as the people dispersed, I sort of lost track of where my team was.

But it didn't matter, as it had been such a wonderful party.

I went back to my cabin and got dressed up for our big eight o'clock show. But when I got to the show, I might as well have heard crickets chirping. Nobody was there! I mean, there was an audience, about a thousand people, in fact.

But no performers were there!

No MC. No deejays. No dancers. Everybody had been wiped out by the beach party. So there I was, dressed to the nines, ready for a big show…and I was the only staff member present at this event.

I wish I could tell you I stood there on stage and did a juggling act, but instead I handed the mic to a couple of guys from my team—not performers—who talked up the crowd, making jokes and engaging in light chitchat. I then ran around the ship as fast as I could.

Aboard these ships, you don't communicate by cell phone. We are overseas, the signals are often bad, and people are more or less unplugged from their electronic devices. So I had to run around finding people.

I'd asked those two guys to hold the crowd over for ten minutes. Well, before we knew it, ten had somehow managed to turn into sixty!

In the meantime, though, I pulled a show together: a handful of dancers, a bleary-eyed deejay, and enough entertainment value to keep the crowd happy and satisfied.

Yet amid all that action, the lesson was clear: no more shows after beach parties!

As much as I enjoy sharing these fun stories, that last one goes hand in hand with a pretty serious point: my staff is worth its weight in gold.

It takes monumental effort to put events like our cruises together, which is why instead of reprimanding everyone for being tired, I adjusted the schedule to avoid having people crash too early.

Think about what it might take to produce the biggest concert in the world. Maybe your task is to entertain twenty thousand people over the course of four hours. If a piece of equipment is broken, it's not tragic. You just go to the nearest supplier and get a replacement. But aboard a cruise ship, you have no such options. You're there for days on end, out at sea, with no local suppliers to run over to if there is a problem. As I said, you don't even have cell phones to communicate with. In addition, you've crammed many technical supplies aboard, all to generate light, sound, color, and energy. To get this equipment there, you've not only had to use physical exertion but you've also had to get through customs and put up with waiting in long lines. Then once you're finally aboard, you have to rush around, in the course of three or four hours, setting everything up so the cruise is ready to go when the guests arrives. Deejay booths, personnel, the whole ADC atmosphere—it all must be ready to go.

Planning a cruise is like planning the ultimate concert, and though I once poured time into trying to do it alone, the whole process has improved with a team of impassioned experts in my corner.

In 2013, we were scheduled to dock at an island. This was one of the cruise's central events. But the cruise line told us the wind was bad, and nobody was getting off that boat: "Safety first." Naturally, ADC is all about "safety first," too, but this also meant hatching a whole new plan on the spot and filling up times on the schedule with deejays and dancers. How much time did we have to accomplish this?

A single hour. That was it!

That we pulled it off is a credit to my excellent team—100 percent.

In 2014, my team shone again under difficult circumstances. We were about to have a huge beach party, and I'd hired a local company to provide lights and speakers. We'd invested a lot of money in that party, and we wanted to create the best event ever to hit that island.

The people I'd hired not only didn't show up on time; they also didn't bring a generator with them. They were responsible for lighting up the area and playing our music from their speakers, and they had no ability to provide power. Fortunately, I'd shown up an hour early to make sure things were OK...which they were not!

So Team ADC sprang into action.

We tried renting a generator, but on a Saturday afternoon in the Bahamas, at the last minute, that was just a little bit challenging. So we approached several business owners around the area, asking to rent their speakers.

We set up those speakers from the local venues and ran long, long cables to the bar we were working with, where the deejays worked with half of their regular equipment, and even though the whole party had a far less polished setup than we'd initially planned for, we managed to make it happen.

Make ship happen, in other words.

That's my team. That's ADC...doing everything we can to keep the dancing and party going.

⟜⟶

People are going to laugh at me for this one...

Or at least I hope they laugh!

On these cruises, in case you haven't noticed, I barely have a moment to breathe. I'm working hard nonstop (and loving it!), and I always have to steal time to accomplish absolutely everything.

As anybody who's been on a cruise ship knows, early on in the voyage, there is a mandatory safety drill. Everybody aboard the boat must attend. If staff members find you wandering around, they literally escort you to a TV monitor and force you to watch the drill. By now, I've watched that drill more times than I can count. I'm such a safety expert that I could give the presentation myself. So every chance I get, when the drill begins, I rush to my cabin and use those thirty minutes to change. For everybody else, it's a safety drill, but for me—it's my time to take a breath and change.

And don't worry about my breaking the rules, because—trust me—those cruise-ship guys always manage to find out I skipped the drill and force me to get all caught up, even though by now I can recite the thing by heart.

To me, it's worth skirting the rules a little to make ship happen. I'm determined to put on an excellent cruise, no matter what it takes.

⸻

Speaking of time management, here's a fun trick I picked up over the years, which I recommend you use when you're on one of our cruises. Room service is almost always free on cruises. The problem is, it takes half an hour or so for the food to arrive. I never have that kind of time on any given day on the cruise. Are you kidding? A free half hour would be like a rare, precious jewel.

So what I've learned to do, before I head out to a given event, is to call room service and order lots of food. I'm talking about burgers, fruit, chicken, salads, cookies—all the stuff I like. Then I go to the event and forget all about it. And let me tell you something: coming back to my cabin at four in the morning and being greeted by that food is like crawling across the desert and then finding a crisp, fresh pool of water. I sit there all alone, on the ocean, in the middle of the night, feasting like a king. Even if I only walk into my cabin for a moment to grab something, it's great to have something to stuff my face with before I leave. After all, sometimes scoring a real chance to eat is pretty much out of the question.

Always order in advance to eliminate your waiting time and have a nice "surprise" waiting for you later on.

Hey, it's not really rocket science.

It's all about making ship happen.

# Fast-Tempo Version

- Develop and nurture the habit of taking risks.
- Break large tasks down into smaller ones: take things one step at a time.
- Know that small accomplishments will set the stage for larger ones.
- Make *ship* happen, every day of your life.

# MEASURING PROGRESS AND THE KEY TO HAPPINESS

*Pleasure can be supported by an illusion;*
*but happiness rests upon truth.*

—SÉBASTIEN-ROCH NICOLAS DE CHAMFORT

Although every chapter in this book is important to me, this one holds a particularly special place in my heart, as the point I'm making here has helped me enormously in terms of my personal happiness and growth.

Through attending seminars, running my own businesses, and just living my life, I've learned that the key to happiness in any form—whether it's business or health or personal relationships—is actually being able to see and measure growth.

That's it! That's the key!

It may sound simple, but just think about it: growth not only makes us happy but also motivates us to keep on going. In fact, I can't think of anything more motivating than seeing results.

Think of how we feel when we don't know how we're doing. We're stuck. We're lost. We're waiting for a change.

On the other hand, think of our mental and emotional attitudes when results are taking place. We're excited. We're inspired. We feel like we have the wind at our sails and momentum in our steps.

Results equal motivation. Motivation equals results.

But here's where things get tricky. Oftentimes, we are actually making progress, but we don't notice it. Why? Because we don't know how to measure progress correctly.

So the key is not only experiencing progress but also knowing how to measure it.

Only when we can see progress happening do we know how to stick with or build upon what we're doing. Meanwhile, if we know how to measure progress but are seeing no progress, then it's time to change up our approach. There's nothing worse, though, than not knowing how to assess our progress and then making an unnecessary change because we felt we were getting no results, even though we actually were.

# THE POWER OF PATIENCE COMBINED WITH PERSISTENCE: THE STORY OF THE CHINESE BAMBOO TREE

Take, for example, Chinese bamboo.

Chinese bamboo provides the perfect example of how we should go about measuring progress. The crazy thing about this bamboo is that it takes years of watering, nurturing, and being patient before it actually begins to show results.

When you plant Chinese bamboo, it's time to embrace as much Zen patience as is humanly possible. First, you plant the seed. Then, day in and day out, you water the soil as attentively and carefully as possible.

For an entire year, you stick to this process.

And nothing happens—nothing, that is, that's visible to the naked eye.

When the second year comes, you keep on watering. You steadily maintain the process. You don't take breaks. You never neglect your precious but unseen Chinese bamboo.

But still, throughout that whole second year, you see zero results.

Then comes the third year, when you've become entirely accustomed to this slow process. Now you attend to the seeds without even thinking about it. The water pitcher ends up in your hand and out you go, watering as naturally as you breathe, walk, or blink.

However, as that third year goes on, still virtually nothing sprouts from the ground. At best, you might see a mere three to five inches of bamboo poking up out of the soil. Neighbors might come over and ask what you're doing. "Planting Chinese bamboo," you say.

"Oh, wonderful!" they answer. "Where is it?"

Then you point to a pathetic patch of dirt outside.

Before you know it, the fourth year arrives. You're as on schedule as you ever were. You water. You keep your eye on the prize. Let your neighbors mock you. Let everybody think you've lost your mind.

Just keep on watering. Because year five is right around the corner.

In year five, after you've put in all that effort, been unbelievably patient, gained more years on your timeline, had countless successes and failures, and seen people come and people go, you finally look at what was once a bare patch of dirt and see *lots of bamboo growing there*!

And when I tell you that you'll see "lots of" bamboo, I don't mean just a modest little stick jutting out of the dirt. I mean that Chinese bamboo actually grows to a height of ninety feet!

It's staggering. It's overwhelming. I can only imagine what it was like to be the first guy who actually planted that bamboo. How in the world did he know that something was actually going to come out of five straight years of watering?

I'm sure his friends thought he was crazy. In fact, I've pondered this a lot, and I'm having trouble believing that he actually *wasn't* crazy. I mean, how does somebody scrape together that kind of faith?

It doesn't matter. It's plain, wild science.

How does the bamboo grow to ninety feet? Simple. During those first four years, the plant was working hard on developing extremely strong and amazingly long roots underneath the ground. Major growth was taking place below the surface, so even though it couldn't be seen, it deserved deep, earnest trust.

Then, when it was finally ready, it sprouted like nothing that anyone could believe. In two to three weeks, legitimate bamboo shot up out of the ground!

See, progress can often be hard to detect. That's why it's so important that we develop an actual scent for it.

On my own path, it certainly took a little while to pick up this skill...

*I'm a great believer in luck, and I find the*
*harder I work, the more I have of it.*

—THOMAS JEFFERSON

In business, for a long time, I had the habit of looking at my income as the main source of progress. I think the same holds true for many businesspeople. If your income is growing monthly or annually, then that's legitimate progress and a sign that things are going well.

While learning how to read corporate financial reports and trade and invest in the stock market, I discovered the many different ways of evaluating companies. Sometimes profits, also known as the bottom line, don't grow, and sometimes there are losses, but if you know how to evaluate a company carefully, you might see that sales did grow in a way. Perhaps, for example, the company has more clients than it did the previous year, which indicates that by simply increasing the rates a bit or adding a new product, the company could show huge profits in the years to come. Or maybe the company is actually only showing a loss because the board of directors decided to buy another company or invest. Maybe the company paid off debts. The point is that, even if this company did show a loss, an experienced onlooker would still be able to identify big and bright signs of potential.

Sometimes your income may not change at all for months or years. Sometimes it might even go in the wrong direction. At times like those, I questioned whether or not I was making progress. But I would have been wrong to throw in the towel, and here's why: sometimes I would have a year with no income growth, but I would look back and see that I'd done other things during that year that were actually moving things forward. Maybe I'd invested. Maybe I'd grown my customer base or upgraded my marketing system.

I had to learn, over time, to measure subtler, nonnumeric things to make sure I was really heading in the right direction. Like with the Chinese bamboo, the things I measured weren't always right in front of my eyes but oftentimes right below the surface.

Going back to the example of investing, what's interesting about good investors is that they're not only concerned with the bottom line. Sure, the bottom line is important to them, but they're also looking at less obvious factors. For example, if a company's sales or customer base is growing over time despite the bottom line remaining more or less the same, that sales and customer growth are still valuable to the investor, for they are actual results. And the investor knows that just modifying costs or upgrading efficiency can bring in more money over time.

The key, then, to measuring progress is to look for genuine forward-moving activity. It doesn't have to be exact or numeric; rather, it just has to be going in the right direction.

In business, I've failed so many times. I don't look at these events as "failures" in the purest sense of that word, though. Instead, see each one as a stepping-stone. Although the dance studio is now in my past, I learned customer service and accounting from it. Although I launched a few websites that aren't around anymore, I learned search-engine optimization and marketing from them. Although I produced a dance DVD that wasn't a smash hit, I learned the process of production from making it. Although I hosted a bunch of events that didn't go on to become classics, I learned event planning from putting those together.

Sure, at the time, I wasn't thrilled (to say the least) with the results I was getting, but when I took a good, close look at the situation, I was more than pleased to see that actual results were always staring right back at me.

This relates to personal relationships, too. When you're in a relationship, you always want to be sure that you're growing with your partner and not stagnating. It's important to be excited about new things. First you get together, and then later you make a commitment, and then you move in together, and then you get engaged, and then comes marriage, buying a house, and maybe having a child, and so on.

Forward motion, again, is the key to happiness. There's no worse feeling than seeing a year go by in which nothing positive or progressive has happened. In relationships, that's why people get so upset when their partners aren't proposing or when they're not open to having children. It's because time is precious, and we want to make the most of the time we have. This goes not only for romantic relationships but also for our family relationships. We want to feel that we're growing and improving in these relationships, rather than repeating the same cycles over and over.

I've also learned that seeing results is incredibly important when it comes to losing weight. But like with money, the numbers here actually aren't everything. Sure, it's important to actually drop the pounds, but what happens later, when you reach a plateau? Does that mean you've failed? Does that mean you are done improving? Not necessarily.

Maybe you've expanded your workout time. Maybe you've increased your speed. Maybe you've even reached a good weight and are now better off focusing on toning and improving your look by losing body fat percentage or increasing muscle mass.

The point, as I have said, is to keep our eyes open for legitimate signs of progress that are subtler than the most obvious ones. For the more signs of progress that we see, the happier we become.

So many famous, successful people are known for always trying to improve. Bill Gates, Steve Jobs, Oprah Winfrey, Walt Disney, Michael Jordan—the list goes on and on. These people are inspiring not only because they look for results but also because they actively seek out and attain results.

I've always done my best to follow these people's good example. When I was at school, I got my bachelor's degree and then went on to my master's. In my first business, I was always working on ways to boost my income and grow my customer base. Now that I have the cruise line, I've gone from booking cruises to chartering ships to chartering even more ships and planning to charter even bigger ships.

The English language, also, was a growth process for me. First, I had to learn how to speak it and then I worked on my public speaking. I got a speech coach. I constantly tried to improve when it came to making presentations and speaking in public.

If ever a month or two goes by during which I haven't read a new book or watched an inspiring movie or picked up some new skill, I swear I start to feel like I'm going crazy! I have to go on Amazon or iTunes, look around, and pick up something that will stimulate my mind.

And note that this isn't about becoming a master. It's not about being the best or crushing the competition. No. It's about remaining open, staying in motion, and attaining true happiness because I'm in a constant state of growth.

I've seen so many people get their college degrees and try to stretch them across a lifetime. But that's not realistic. You have to constantly keep doing better. Before you know it, that degree will get old and dusty. The world is changing so fast nowadays. Technology, the way we communicate, the way we do business—everything. If you think your education gave you all you need to know, you're going to fall behind pretty fast.

By being open, learning, and seeking results, you always can ensure that you'll stay ahead of the game.

*If you think education is expensive, try ignorance!*

—DEREK BOK

When we study dancing, we all start out as beginners and have to put time into learning the basics. Then the next step is intermediate, followed by advanced dancing. Along the way, we start traveling. We dance in public. We experience new teachers. We conquer new challenges.

But what's next?

Among all the dancers whom I know, I've heard it repeated time and time again that if you dance over a long period of time, something significant happens around two or three years into the process. This is something that is hard to explain in words.

After all that practice, all those classes, all the socials and partners and situations, something finally just clicks. You finally feel more comfortable on the dance floor. You gain a more natural link to the music and the rhythms, and as a result you start getting more creative. The reason for this is that you become comfortable. The steps are a part of you; you don't have to even think about them. You start listening to the music, to the lyrics. You start even focusing on the instruments and anticipating every break in the song. You are now having a new kind of fun. You are in the "zone."

Then, if you stay the course of learning and practicing, you find that you can just keep growing and growing. You can always change up the exact same step in ten or twenty different ways. As you go on, you get smoother. You vary your posture. Your smile. Your attitude. Your styling.

You also change depending on the song that's playing: its speed, sound, rhythm, texture, tone, and emotion. No matter what it is, you can apply a style that fits it and expresses something as only you can.

To me, it's amazing how different people can all take the same class, learn the same steps, and execute the same dance moves, yet be so drastically—yet beautifully—different from one another. We're all unique and all naturally here to express a different story.

My point is this: If you are not growing, you are dying. The possibilities are endless. And since that's the case, the opportunities for growth and expansion are endless, too.

We can, therefore, always exist in a state of progress.

Pasta is pasta, sure, but it changes a tremendous amount depending on what you put on it. Different sauces. Different spices. Different whatever. It's no different in dancing: you can vary the same theme in a zillion different ways.

It can go on forever.

I can go on about this topic forever because it excites me to my core. But just in case I haven't yet convinced you, here are my five main reasons you should measure progress:

1. Measuring progress keeps you motivated.
2. Measuring progress shows you growth or a lack of growth.

3. Measuring progress allows you to make adjustments. Information and knowledge translate into power. Regardless, actions you take will ultimately help you grow.
4. Measuring progress is simply *fun*. I always tell people it's like a game, and I'm in it because I want to earn more points—except the things I get out of this game are way better than points.
5. Measuring progress gives you practice at setting goals. The more practice you get, the more you get used to setting goals and the more you can achieve.

*A goal without a plan is just a wish.*

—Antoine de Saint-Exupery

As you make your way along the path of measuring progress, always get advice from professional people with experience. After all, what's the point of asking advice from people who never did the thing that you're trying to do? I mean, your bachelor friend might love you and want the best for you, but he's not exactly qualified to give you relationship advice.

However, keep in mind that an experienced person doesn't necessarily have to be a successful person. As we know, experience often leads to failure. But in every case, no matter what the result was, experience is better than no experience.

So I like talking to people who have failed as well as those who have succeeded because I like to find out what they did wrong, so I don't repeat the same mistakes that they made.

With that in mind, maybe it's not such a bad idea to listen to your bachelor friend after all. If he's a bachelor who just got dumped, maybe you should listen and find out why. That way, when you're trying to keep your own relationship intact, you don't do what that guy did.

Failures—both our own and those of others—can often be incredibly valuable when it comes to our making progress and scoring results.

And never forget that the more progress you make and the better you are at measuring it, the more happiness will inevitably come your way.

# Fast-Tempo Version

- **The key to happiness is growing and being able to measure progress.**
- **Remember how Chinese bamboo grows: results are not always in plain sight.**
- **Failures are just successes in work clothes.**
- **Chances to progress exist all around us; we simply have to be ready to acknowledge and seize them.**
- **Study people who have succeeded at what you'd like to accomplish (as well as those who have failed)!**

# THE "RIGHT" TURN

*Life is like dancing. If we have a big floor, many people will dance. Some will get angry when the rhythm changes. But life is changing all the time.*

—DON MIGUEL RUIZ

In dancing, at the beginning of our training, we learn all about certain turns. There is the right turn. There is the left turn. Our feet carry us this way and that.

However, in reality, there is no "right" turn—meaning there is never really any correct direction to go in. In other words, we need to accept and embrace the fact that things change, all the time. When we stand at a fork in the road, it really makes no difference whether we go left or right, because, eventually, down the path we choose, changes will come, and we will have to deal with them.

So this part of the book is about embracing change and using it as a tool to move forward in the best way possible. The truth is that change happens regardless of whether we want it to or not, so in order to grow, it's best to accept change and learn to live with it.

A key part of improving and growing is accepting change.

*We plan, God laughs.*

—Old Yiddish Proverb

# My Enough Moment

Over the years, I have learned the power of something that I like to call the "enough moment." This is the moment when you've had enough. This is the moment when your circumstances just can't be tolerated any longer. When you reach your enough moment, you can no longer accept the way things are, and you just have to change them.

This, of course, is the very essence of embracing change.

How long does it take to quit smoking? Or get off drugs or decide to lose weight? How long does it take to meet your significant other? Or to conquer any other goal that's been pressing on you?

I'll tell you how long: it takes a moment. A split second.

That's it.

It's not a process that stretches on for weeks or months or years or even hours. It just takes a single, simple moment. It's the concept of "the straw that broke the camel's back." Maybe it comes in the form of a comment that somebody makes. Maybe it's a situation that you find yourself stuck in. Whatever it is, it causes you to throw your hands up and say, "That's it. I'm done! This will not happen again!"

Whatever you're letting go of was serving you at one time. You felt good about smoking or taking drugs. You were happy being single, at least on some level. But when your enough moment finally strikes, you cannot tolerate the way things are for another moment. Then, you actually have to force yourself to make the change.

And by that point, it doesn't really feel like forcing yourself, because you now want the change more than you want things to stay the same.

Sure, many days and nights and hours led up to that enough moment, but when it comes down to it, it's just a moment. Nobody goes broke overnight or becomes overweight overnight. When businesses fail, they generally don't fail because of just one bad decision. No, it takes time for things to accumulate, just like with the Chinese bamboo we talked about before.

But eventually, my friends, it's a moment.

I know, 'cause I have been there.

There I was, an ambitious young guy in my midtwenties, owning a business in the United States of America.

I'd been through a whole journey. I'd gotten my bachelor's degree, followed by my master's. I'd worked for other people, and then I'd taken the leap and started my own dance studio.

From one side of me came grave warnings: "Don't do it; you're bound to fail."

From the other side of me came warm encouragement: "You're a rock star! A superstar! Nothing can stop you!"

Amid all the chatter and crisscrossed opinions, I got established as a businessperson. I was the "real thing," going about my business day to day.

But I was not thriving.

Nobody knew the truth about how I was doing. Back home, many of my relatives were singing my praises. I was the big shot who'd gone to America, gotten degrees, mastered a new language and culture, and was generally kicking ass.

However, in reality, I was scraping by. I had bills piling up. I kept experimenting with new and different services to bring in fresh sources of income. On some level, I couldn't be blamed because in the Great Recession economy, everyone was struggling. However, I didn't want to be one of those people who blamed his situation on the economy.

I knew that somehow, some way, I could find the key to improving my situation, but as each new day came, I just found myself stuck—spinning my wheels.

My big "enough moment" finally came when I wanted to buy a plane ticket home, to go visit my family. It was an entirely natural and common instinct, something people experience every second of every day.

Yet, when I got on the Internet and started scrolling through flight options, reality hit me:

I couldn't even afford a plane ticket.

You would think that a big-shot American businessman would have no problem booking a flight to go see his family, but there I was, without the cash to do so.

Let me tell you: it was a crushing moment.

It wasn't like I lost control of my emotions, but in truth, this subtle, quiet episode screamed the word "enough" right in my face.

You never know where these moments will come from. They certainly have a way of sneaking up on you...

In my case, the shame of not being able to buy that ticket had amazing force behind it. I was tired of just scraping by. I was sick of being a second-tier businessperson. I was embarrassed that on some level, despite my fancy studio and menu of services, I was like so many other people around me: living month to month, at best.

That wasn't what I'd come to America for. Nor was it what I'd studied so hard to accomplish. Nor was it what I'd opened my own business for.

Something had to change—and now.

I'd had *enough.*

What's interesting is that, when you hit your enough moment, you usually realize that it's not just one problem that's holding you back. Instead, you see that your whole way of life really isn't working right then.

In my case, when I had my enough moment, I was overweight, far from being fit, single, and not really thriving at the art of dancing. I'd just struggled to get my hands on a visa so I could finally travel home, but then I couldn't even afford the ticket.

This is why it's so important to understand that there is no "right" turn. When you have your enough moment, it's not as simple as saying, "Oh, I'll just do *x*, *y*, or *z*, and then everything will magically be different."

Nuh-uh—it doesn't work that way.

Real change has to come from within. It starts with the right mind-set and attitude. I didn't get out of my situation just by saying, "I'll start offering new kinds of services, and then I'll have more money and be able to buy a plane ticket."

It's not that simple.

My change had to come on every level. I had to get thinner and healthier. I had to work on becoming more appealing to potential female partners. I had to dig in and get more serious about dancing to better to uphold my position as an expert in my art form. I had to become a better and smarter businessman, get more tools, and build a better team around me.

In other words, it wasn't all about money or a plane ticket. It was about the way I was approaching things on a day-to-day level.

All of it finally had to change.

For change to be meaningful, it has to be deep.

And when change is deep, *everything* changes.

*If you want something you've never had,*
*you must be willing to do something you've never done.*

—THOMAS JEFFERSON

When I learned how to dance, I learned it on a social level. I never aimed to be a pro.

I remember that when I was just starting out, it took me a long time to drum up the courage to ask women to dance with me. I had this voice inside my head telling me that I wasn't ready and that I wasn't good enough. But looking back, I see now that I should have just gone in more quickly. It's like when you start your first business: you know the first thing you try probably won't succeed, so you should just dive in and get it over with.

*Just Do It.*

—NIKE

There was this one woman on the scene whom I really wanted to dance with. She was a great dancer, good looking, and she always caught my eye.

So one night, I built up the courage to approach her, and I asked her to dance. What's the worst that could happen, right? She'd say no?

Well, as it turned out, her saying no wasn't the worst that could happen.

She said yes and danced with me, but halfway through the dance, she stopped and didn't want to finish. She gave me some lame excuse, but I knew exactly why she left.

Aw, poor Moshe…

What's interesting about this is that in the world of dancing, what she did was actually bad manners. Advanced social dancers and dance instructors should always know to grant dances to students and beginners, as a way of being courteous and giving them another chance to practice. As a matter of fact, when I got better, I looked forward to dancing with beginners. Making them look good was a great challenge for me. Anyone can dance with a pro and look good, but it's not that easy the other way around. Anyway, I didn't even know that at the time, so it's not like I was counting on her acceptance, but in hindsight, I guess that maybe she wasn't so advanced after all, at least not in terms of this polite little custom.

The bottom line, though, was that she rejected me.

I wasn't heartbroken. I didn't go home and cry myself to sleep. But it was a fork in the road of sorts. I could easily have said, right then, "Ah, you know what? I'm done. This isn't for me."

Or, alternatively, I could have said, "Oh yeah? Watch this! I am going to change that."

In other words, I was not going to be the guy who got turned down.

Which one do you think I chose?

⌒

Three years went by.

I was at the same venue: an iconic social in South Florida. Everybody was dancing, including that woman who had walked away from our dance. I hadn't planned on being in the same place as she, but there she was.

She looked over at me, several times, saw me doing my thing.

Then she came up to me and asked me to dance. At first, I didn't even recognize her.

I looked at her. Of course, I accepted her dance. We had a nice time dancing, and when it was over, she said to me, "Oh my God! That was great! Oh my God! You're amazing!"

I should stress that it's not like I was some master dancer. I had simply evolved to the point where I knew what I was doing. I had fun. I was confident. I smiled.

In addition, I wasn't out for revenge. I didn't lean over and whisper, "Three years ago, you were a bitch!" after we finished dancing.

Just knowing that she had sought me out and then enjoyed the dance and praised me afterward was plenty. I said to myself, "Wow! I got it!"

It was confirmation from the universe that I'd made the "right" turn and embraced a positive change. The way I felt that day was priceless.

Even when you're down, things can turn around.

And being open to change is the best way to turn things around.

# FAST-TEMPO VERSION

- **Things change all the time.**
- **Be open to and accepting of *all* change.**
- **Big changes generally come down to big moments.**
- **When you seize your *enough moment*, you will turn things around.**

# THE FAITHFUL DANCER

*I've had a lot of worries in my life,*
*most of which never happened.*

—MARK TWAIN

I'm not a particularly spiritual person. It's not that I don't believe in something greater than me; rather that I'm a believer in the power of hard work when it comes to getting where you want to go. That said, hard work isn't the whole equation. So it's also important to have legitimate faith.

Going back to the example of the Chinese bamboo, think of how much faith is required when we wait for that plant to grow. But let's widen our focus a little bit: think of how much faith is needed when we wait for *any* plant to grow.

Sure, we can put in plenty of hard work. We can prep the soil. Plant the seeds. Ensure proper exposure to sunlight. Water the soil every day. But beyond that—we're in nature's hands. And we have to have genuine faith in nature's wisdom.

It's the same thing with everything else we do, from having babies to starting businesses. Yes, we can put in plenty of strong, assertive effort, but after a certain point, no matter what we're up to, it's eventually out of our hands.

The fact that we don't have control shouldn't give us the option of shrugging our shoulders. We shouldn't say, "Oh, well, I tried the best I could. And now I'll wait."

That is the *wrong* attitude to have!

The right outlook is the following: "I planned as well as I could. I put the work in. I'm not attached to every little detail of the outcome. And, therefore, I feel confident that everything's going to work out just fine."

See the difference? The first mind-set is passive, but the second is active. The first one is weak, but the second is strong. And that second one is always the mentality you find in successful people.

When I started my dance studio and, later, my event/cruise company, I had no clue where any of it was headed. The same is true for my decision to come to the United States to pursue citizenship and my higher education. I was completely clueless as to how any of it would turn out. I didn't have some magical pair of glasses that allowed me to get a nice, clean look at the outcome. Instead, I had to hustle, struggle, work, and trust, day after day after day, that things would come together.

Which they did.

And still, as of now, I hustle, struggle, work, and trust, as I pursue a whole new set of outcomes. ADC routinely sets out to make history, but that doesn't mean we write the history books before we set sail. Just like you can't put the cart before the horse, you can't write the story before it's over. The best you can do is live out the story with a deep faith that things will go well.

I've encountered too many people who are stuck because they don't know what kinds of outcomes await them. Such a person resists taking a single step until he or she is absolutely certain of what's waiting around the corner. But the bad news is that nobody gets to know that information. I don't care how many psychics you hire: you don't get a free pass that lets you set out to accomplish something with full knowledge of how it will work out.

With that in mind, your ability to work hard and your faith that things will work out in the end are your best weapons. Optimism has a way of making uncertainty into its bitch. Yes, life is unpredictable by its very nature, but optimists simply do not care. They'll find the good in whatever happens. Rainy day? So what? It's a reason to stay inside and dance—or, even better, dance in the rain!

In dancing, one key thing we learn from the beginning is how to shift our full body weight from one leg to the other. Not only do we have to learn how to do it but we also have to learn how to do it with confidence.

This is something that cannot be accomplished halfway. Literally, it's an all-or-nothing situation. We need to put the entirety of our weight—every last pound of it—onto either one leg or the other.

And when we master this element of dancing, styling comes more naturally, our bodies move more fluidly from top to bottom, and we feel all-around wonderful.

That's because shifting our body weight calls for real confidence. It's almost like that game of trust we played as children, where one kid would close his or her eyes and fall backward, with full faith that the others would be there to catch him or her.

When we shift our body weight, though, we have only ourselves to "catch" us. This is something that our partners cannot do for us. We're on our own, and we need to trust in our own bodies.

Before we finally master this move, we have to study, we have to practice, and we have to experiment and fail. After all that, we're armed with skill and knowledge. Yet beyond all the skill and knowledge in the world, there is still a need for faith.

It goes back to the examples of planting a garden and starting a business. At a certain point, nature just takes over. Thought won't help us. Hope won't help us. Worry won't help us.

But faith will most certainly be our friend and help to keep us moving forward. It's like walking. Can you walk on the street without shifting your full body weight from one leg to the other? Imagine trying that. How far would you get? Furthermore, picture trying to get out of bed in the morning without feeling confident that there is solid ground underneath you. You don't have to think about it; you just know it's there.

Here's a definition of entrepreneurship from Harvard Business School: "Entrepreneurship is the pursuit of opportunity without regard to resources currently controlled." In other words, entrepreneurship is the pursuit of opportunities without knowing the exact resources available to us (that is, how we will get there). Find the *why*, and the *how* will present itself later.

The bottom line is, have faith, be confident, and keep moving forward.

If you're a dancer, the next time you attempt something hard, think about shifting your body weight. You likely didn't get it perfect the first time you tried, probably not even close. However, in the end, as you put in more work, things worked out all right, and you found yourself "luckier."

Most of the time, things actually do work out fine.

And that's reason enough to be faithful, no matter what.

# IF YOU DANCE, THEY WILL COME

It's interesting how even though we can't see exactly how things will turn out, the more we behave as though they'll turn out well, the more they usually do turn out well.

The creation of ADC was a total "if you dance, they will come" moment in my history. I'd worked so hard for so long, but not necessarily with the intention of launching a dance cruise. Regardless, when I planned the very first cruise, I tackled it with as much solid planning and hard work as I tackled anything else. Then, with faith · in my heart, I just let go. We'd put the word out, and we then awaited reservations.

The fact that we got so many was a major life lesson.

I had to put the preconditions in place. The bed had to be warm before someone could lie down in it. If you build it, they will come…

It's easy to fall into the trap of reversing this wisdom. You can think, "I don't want to build it unless I'm sure they will come." This, of course, is when you get stuck.

The key here is to fake it till you make it. The best way to guarantee that no woman will dance with you is to never ask a lady to dance. Me? My philosophy, in so many things, is that it's better to apologize than to ask permission.

The guy on the sidelines who's waiting for someone to ask *him* to dance is essentially asking for permission. The guy who doesn't want to build it unless he's got a thousand RSVPs first is asking for permission.

The guy who just goes ahead and builds it is the guy worth watching.

He's got some serious faith and confidence.

# The Miracle of Dancing

*There are only two ways to live your life. One
is as though nothing is a miracle. The other
is as though everything is a miracle.*

—Albert Einstein

Einstein was right. (What's new?)

There's really no middle ground between optimism and pessimism. Some people try to be cute and call themselves "realists," but "realist" is just another word for "pessimist."

Realists accept reality as they see it, while optimists go ahead and change reality to the way they want it to be. So the next time somebody says that he or she is not a pessimist and is just a realist, ask why he or she is not busy making reality better.

When you get into the habit of—to paraphrase Einstein—seeing everything as a miracle, then you're operating on an extremely positive level. You are grateful all the time, which is extremely powerful. You'll see miracles everywhere you look. A bird on a fence will seem miraculous. Simple laughter will seem like magic. Some people will insist that you're crazy, but you can just let them go ahead and continue being sane. (Yeah, good luck with that!)

I could never have imagined my life turning out the way it has. I'm not talking about the fact that it's positive, because I have always tried to keep a positive outlook. I mean the way it looks and feels. Seeing the positive in everything is a habit worth developing—more than a habit, it's a valuable gift and skill. I'm talking about spending all those glorious days and nights out at sea, upon a boat that my own team has chartered, dancing in a way that nobody else throughout history has ever danced before.

What happened here? I'm no magician. I'm no Albert Einstein. But what I have in common with Einstein is that I look around me and see only miracles. And the more miracles I see, the more miracles seem to come my way.

At its core, dancing is a way of creating miracles. It's a form of "silent poetry." It's a celebration of motion—of the body's movement. Moreover, it's a celebration of sound and how wonderful sounds can inspire wonderful movements. These things do not make conscious sense.

You cannot put into words why a specific song or dance is so moving and exciting.

It just is—because it's a form of miracle. It goes beyond explanation. It's bigger than our understanding.

It's so big that we can only call it a miracle.

# Fast-Tempo Version

- **Have faith that things will work out (because they usually do).**
- **Know that as hard as you work at something, at a certain point, the universe just takes it from there.**
- **It's better to apologize than to ask for permission.**
- **Witness the miracles all around you ('cause they're there)!**

# DANCE WITH YOUR HEART

*People rarely succeed unless they have*
*fun in what they are doing.*

—DALE CARNEGIE

Nothing bothers me more than when I hear people say there's no money in the profession in which I make my living. Clearly, if there's no money in this business and I'm actually succeeding at it, something must be wrong!

Not just that, but everywhere I turn, people tell me that there's no money in dancing or "salsa." Usually, I hear this from my competitors or other people in the industry. Every time somebody brings this up, I say to myself, "Yeah, but when was the last time you looked at yourself in the mirror? Looked at your own work? Evaluated your actions?"

In other words, it's not just "dancing" that does or does not make money. Rather, it's the people who provide (or fail to provide) the dancing-related services.

First and foremost, when you like what you do and you have passion, enthusiasm, and real care backing up your actions, *you will succeed.* Yes, I truly believe that's the case. No, scratch that—I truly know that's the case.

I've found that what sets ADC apart is that we *care*. And it goes beyond mere caring—we actually care *a lot*, which is the key. Every day, we work on improving the little things in our company, figuring out new ways to surprise people and coming up with new ways to make a difference in our field. It's so easy to do this, because we love what we do.

When somebody calls us, we make certain we call them back. I know that doesn't sound like rocket science, but, hey, think about all the times you've called a business for help and never received a callback. Or maybe you did receive a callback, but it was way too late. I don't know about you, but I find that annoying. When I'm in the position of a customer, I like to be taken care of. Customers aren't just people spending money. They want have their needs met and want that experience to be as smooth, painless, and even as enjoyable as possible.

So a huge part of caring in our business is just paying attention to the customer, which means actually opening our ears and our minds and listening to what it is that he or she wants. This isn't easy, no matter who you are. Human beings are sensitive creatures, and we don't always want to make ourselves vulnerable to hearing other people's feedback. But when you're in business, you can't exist in a bubble. You have no other choice but to find out what your customers are looking for, even if that means asking them to share with you where you're falling short. I personally love that part. It makes it so easy for me to know what to fix, as it takes all the guesswork out of the picture.

Once you get feedback from your customers, it's on you to take it in, evaluate it, and do what's necessary to keep improving. I'll give you an example of a case when this happened with us at ADC.

We used to put on shows that were too lengthy. Our performance slots would run for three or four hours, and as a result, we actually lost some quality and our audience got too tired. It was tricky to figure this out at first, as I'm really into overdelivering. I like to exceed expectations and pile on *more*. But here was a case when more was actually turning out to be less. We were so busy stuffing our schedule with shows that we didn't have enough time to tune in and pay close attention to the caliber of the shows themselves, much less the overall experience for the audience. As a result, our shows became hit or miss. One performer would knock 'em dead, but then a couple of others would leave murky impressions.

I have a rule of thumb: whenever we hear the same comment three times, good or bad, we need to do something about it. It's a sign to make a change, whether that means losing something that's bad or enhancing something that's good.

A lot of people began to complain about how long the shows were. Now, when it comes to customer service, you'll always have people with unusual requests and concerns. At ADC, we try to cater to everyone, but sometimes we know that a given person's issue is personal and doesn't reflect our whole customer base. However, in the case of these packed three- to four-hour shows, bad feedback began to creep in from several directions. We started reading e-mail comments with a critical tone. We noticed that the long shows weren't getting much love on our customer-satisfaction surveys.

The bad businessperson, when faced with this kind of input, might lock up and say, "No, those people are wrong! Our shows are great! We're perfect! Can't make everyone happy! Don't change anything!"

Think of how many bad businesses (not to mention dance events) you've seen come and go, ones that were insistent on keeping their own ineffective policies in place despite customers growing irritated, bored, and even angry with them.

But at ADC, that's not how we roll. (Or should I say, "how we cruise." Ha-ha.) Caring is everything with us. So now we have a rule of thumb that no matter what, our shows end within two hours. This gives people more concentrated entertainment at a faster speed and of a higher quality. It also allows our guests more time to enjoy their dinner before the shows begin or to get ready for the nonstop action after the shows are done.

Taken one by one, these little touches may seem minor, but the magnitude of caring enough to make subtle adjustments should not be underestimated. And keep in mind, I not only look for feedback from the customers. I also seek out feedback from the crew, staff, dancers, and cruise line—everyone.

I remember some of the people on our deejay staff started complaining that we didn't have enough musical variety. This wasn't just some expression of the staff members' tastes, though. They were pointing out that we should be offering our clientele more kinds of music. Having been a deejay myself, I have great respect for the job, understand its importance, and get how a good deejay really connects with his or her crowd. So I went to work on hiring more deejays, and not just good ones—the best ones. Now our cruises are designed in such a way that we have different subtypes of playing music in various places on the ship at all times. You want salsa? We got it. Bachata? We got it. Hip-hop? Why not? Merengue? Of course! Top forty? Yes, of course, whatever you want!

The upgrade led to more creative satisfaction on the part of the deejays, more overall pleasure for the guests, and, above all else, a better dance experience! It was a win-win, any way you sliced it.

All the time, people tell me they loved their vacation with us, but to be honest, that comment doesn't mean a lot to me anymore. It's not that I'm ungrateful for the positive feedback. Instead, it's that I'm eager to find out why they liked it. So I'm always asking them, "Why? Why? Why?"

It's one thing to accept good feedback and go off patting yourself on the back even though you don't know exactly what the person liked. But it's another thing entirely to engage with the person telling you what he or she thinks and figure out what he or she is actually saying.

So I make mental notes when I'm listening to people's reactions: You like the deejays? Great! Our attention to detail? Noted! Our fast responses? Awesome!

The more our customers like something, the more we value it and the more we provide it to the people we serve.

To any promoters in my business who think your clients are clueless and are not paying attention to the little things, I'm here to tell you just how wrong you are. In fact, the biggest mistake you can make as a businessperson is to underestimate your customers' intelligence—which, of course, is just another way of not caring. When you misjudge people and cut corners, your event will be just like everybody else's: mediocre, forgettable, and unsatisfying. But when you open your eyes and see that the customer is a thinking, feeling human being with actual, legitimate concerns, you will work as hard as you possibly can to serve that person.

Oh, and just like you wouldn't mess with a woman's dress and makeup, don't try and mess with dancers' music or dance floor either—deejays and all!

'Cause they know exactly what they want.

No matter what you're selling, if you're the one selling it, then part of your job is to understand its value and importance to the person who is buying. You have to bear in mind that the people who are buying your product or service want to feel special, taken care of, and supported. That's just part of human nature. It has been proven over and over again in many studies surveying employees that they do not place salary at the top of their list of priorities. Feeling special, important, appreciated, taken care of, and supported is far more important to them.

And the same goes, of course, for customers.

The way I look at it, when people are giving ADC their hard-earned money that will allow them to spend their vacation with us, they are granting us a major honor. They have plenty of reasons not to spend their money, their time, and their vacation with us. They have numerous other vacation options. When they choose us, we have to make sure they know they made the perfect choice, for each and every second of their voyage. That means caring. It means taking care of them.

It means rewarding their monetary investment with the gift of value: an experience they will never forget.

Nothing dampens my day more than walking into a store where the products are cheap and feeling like I'm not receiving any attention from the employees. Sure, the prices might be low, but where in the world are the employees who are supposed to help? And why in the world am I waiting in such a long line before I can finally check out? Don't they value my time?

There is a saying in sales: "The bitterness of a poor deal lingers much longer then the happiness of a good deal."

Businesses that reel people in with low prices will always be able to draw some customers to them, but the values and priorities of these businesses are often in the wrong place. They may offer bargains, but they don't necessarily offer heart. I personally would much rather go to a store where my confidence is inspired and my needs are met than to one where I'm left wandering across a vast desert of bad attitudes and sloppy aisles, even if it means paying a few dollars more for products that I could get cheaper somewhere else.

Part of the reason for my success is that I am—and always will be—a customer first. When I rent a home, I want the landlord to be attentive and professional. When I order a meal, I want the details taken care of and the delivery to be swift. Therefore, when the tables are turned, and I'm the one responsible for serving customers, you better believe I'm going to give it my very best shot.

"By dancers, for dancers."

ADC often uses those four words to describe itself. In other words, we're not just business people making money (which is certainly nothing to be ashamed of) but rather, we are an actual, legitimate part of the dancing scene. The art scene. The creative scene. The good people scene.

In other words, if you're looking for a place to dance, then we know exactly what you are looking for. I like saying that we are Disneyland for dancers. And just like Walt, we are not just thinking about the kids (dancers). We are thinking about the whole family.

This expertise extends not only to our clients but also to our performers. When our performers arrive at the terminal, we greet them with a letter that spells out their precise requirements throughout the course of the cruise. It simply makes all our work easier. Then, when they're hard at work aboard the boat, they're treated to a fully catered backstage area. If you've ever performed, you know that you often don't have time to eat before the show, so just knowing that when you get offstage, after you stretch and get out of your costume, you'll have food waiting for you is sheer heaven. The words of praise we receive about that touch alone are enough to keep us busy all year long.

Knowing what social dancing is all about means understanding the precise needs of dancers. As another example, when you're throwing parties, flashing lights in the ceiling may look cool, but for dancers, they are not a good thing. Dancers need to be able to see their partners, grab their hands, telegraph their next moves, and so on. A dark, flashy room won't really serve them all that well. So from the dance floors to the speed of the music to the food backstage to the water offstage, we treat our dancers as well as possible, which pays off tremendously when it comes to the paying customers.

Speaking of those customers, I could fill a whole book with the generous words in their letters and e-mails.

"I had the time of my life."

"You guys reignited my passion for dancing."

"I met my best friend on your cruise."

And on and on…

But there's one particular e-mail I will never forget. I won't share the name of the woman who sent it, but I will tell a little bit about her story here. In the months leading up to her ADC vacation, she had been to hell and back. Her mother had passed away. She had lost her job. One of her kids had gotten into an accident. Basically, if her letter didn't make you cry, then you were probably made of stone. But despite all she'd been through, she was determined to follow through on her ADC cruise. And you know what? The cruise gave her a jolt of energy and power. She said that her experience with us was the only thing that could help her disconnect from her problems, forget about all the bad stuff, be happy again, and just dance! She had more fun than she could have ever imagined, and she made plans to come again the following year.

Speaking of energy and power, letters like that one that clarify ADC's mission for the team members all over again. Reading that letter made me feel such an intense sense of purpose, it inspired me to double down on my mission. For as long as we possibly can, we are going to keep hitting the ocean, keep playing the music, keep throwing our unique and amazing parties, keep on transforming as many lives as possible, and most importantly... keep on *dancing*!

As the years go by, one goal I'm working hard at perfecting is remembering every single guest's name. Do you think I can do it? Well, I'm trying my best. It's not easy when you're gathering together a couple of thousand family members (or more), but then again, who wants things to be easy? (Wink.)

At ADC, I will never see a certain guest as Customer #4371. I will instead see Mr. James Garcia and his lovely wife, Pam, and I will do my best to discover what brought them aboard and find out how I can make their journey even better, or like Disney said, make them want to come back and bring their friends.

No matter who you are, where you are from, what you look like, or whom you love, the ADC family takes you seriously and has ample room for your presence.

If you're young and just want to party and go crazy—fine! We provide that. If you're a more mature dancer and want to attend stellar workshops to refine your craft—sure! We provide that. If you're a pro dancer who's out to network, keep up with old friends, be inspired by great shows, and even go a little crazy at night—wonderful! We provide that. If you're a seasoned veteran who just wants to keep your dancing flame alight and are searching for another way to do so—well, I have two words for you, "All aboard!"

Now, I don't like to play favorites when it comes to my customers, because it's kind of like a father choosing his favorite children, but let me take a moment and share the touching story of one of my all-time favorite groups of customers who ever booked a cruise with ADC.

I'm talking about my own family.

The cruise had been up and running for several years before they decided to join us. For me, this was extremely exciting, as they now could finally see for themselves what I'd been talking so much about. Also, I think my dad's decision to come on the cruise finally gave him a chance to fully understand what I do. After all, it had taken me years to be able to explain quickly to people what I did in a few words. People would ask me, and I'd sort of freeze up. Was I an event promoter? Not exactly. Was I a dance instructor? Well, not really...

"I produce Latin-dance cruises" is one handy way of putting it.

But they would still have a lot of questions for me after that.

"A cruise?"

"That's all?"

"Sail a ship?"

"Only a weekend?"

"That's all you do?"

"And what about the rest of the year?"

I would just shake my head.

So if it was hard for me, and I was actually the guy doing it, imagine how hard it was for my dad to explain it to other people. I'm sure he'd been out on the green with his golfing buddies and they'd asked about how I was doing. He had probably muttered something along the lines of, "Oh, Moshe? He dances on a boat... um...it's a party...shows or something...yeah."

This is not to say my dad wasn't proud of me. On the contrary, he's always been my biggest cheerleader. But let me tell you, when he came aboard that ship and saw the magnitude of the operation, I think it split his mind wide open.

In the meantime, it was so moving to see how much respect the cruise executives gave him. They treated him like he was their superior. They even threw me a small appreciation party one night, with a cake and a toast to our success. For my dad, who's kind of old school, to see these cruise-ship fellas decked out in white and acting so official, all for the sake of supporting his son's business—well, it was hard not to get a little lump in my throat.

For me, that moment was just another payoff for all the loving care I had poured into ADC. Throughout all those many years, I'd thought of the customer, I'd thought of the mission, and, of course, I'd thought of my own well-being. But to see the operation through my dad's eyes exposed me to a whole new level of it.

I realized that I had been blessed to build something of great depth and meaning—and that is truly worth caring for.

# Fast-Tempo Version

- Heart is *everything.*
- Caring is *everything.*
- The only way to give people what they want is to care enough to find out what they want, at a deep level.
- See the world through other people's eyes (and stop assuming), and you will witness something beautiful!

# OWN YOUR DANCE FLOOR

*You are the average of the five people you spend*
*the most time with, including yourself.*

—JIM ROHN

I'll get right to the point: choose where you dance.

In other words, you alone are responsible for declaring the shape, size, and boundaries of your personal spot on the dance floor. Whether you dance in the middle of the dance floor or at the edges or even out there in the seats or on the carpet (those of you who attend congresses know what I mean) is all up to you. As long as you have the right venue and space and good surroundings, you're set.

This part of the book is about setting clear boundaries in terms of your time and energy as well as in terms of whom and what you surround yourself with. As you make better choices in these areas, you can manage to exist more effectively and efficiently.

There is a clear link between your lifestyle, on all levels, and how productive and satisfied you feel.

Thus, it's incredibly important to take ownership of your dance floor.

Over the years, I've come to learn that when you don't keep track of your lifestyle, you can easily lose balance. Stress can overtake you. Suddenly, you're no longer in charge of your time, you're not effective, you're not efficient, you're letting each day slip right through your grasp, and before you know it, even when you manage to do your work—or anything else that's important to you—you're not capable of giving it your all.

That was pretty much a summary of who I had become.

So step by step, inch by inch, I started taking a good look around my own personal dance floor.

For starters, let's focus on technology. Phones, tablets, computers—all these devices can be wonderful tools, but they had started turning into my sworn enemies. I wasn't controlling them; instead, they were controlling me. So I had to develop discipline in terms of when to use my phone and when to put it on silent. Certain times of the day became devoted to work, which meant that any distractions had to be sidelined.

It wasn't just my phone, though, that was driving me to distraction. It was e-mail, too. All day long, I was getting hammered by e-mails. I wanted to always stay on top of everything, so I checked and replied to them right as they came in. Big mistake!

I came to realize that checking my e-mails once or twice a day and taking care of everything at once was much more effective than being a slave to my e-mail and checking it every five minutes. I once heard a business expert say that checking your e-mail all the time is like constantly going to your front door, peeking outside, and saying, "Is anybody coming?"

In other words, it's ridiculous, a waste of time.

My meetings and phone calls were getting crazy, too. It became clear that a fast, tight thirty-minute phone call was often far more effective and valuable than a sprawling, repetitive sixty-minute phone call. I started showing up to all meetings with a clear, precise agenda, knowing exactly what I wanted, as opposed to appearing casually, finding my way on the spot, and wasting precious moments that could be spent on other things.

As I embraced these measures, I naturally realized that certain things were beyond my control. But that was OK, because a big part of managing stress is accepting what you can take charge of and working on it and realizing that there's no use in worrying about what you can't control, because that would just frustrate and derail you.

Something else that took me time to get good at was making better use of my mornings (more on this in the next section). For a long time, I never woke up early, had breakfast, or spent any time taking care of myself before launching into my busy day.

So like building a muscle, I had to develop discipline. The ability to exercising self-control is never just handed to you; rather it's always something that you have to learn and earn. When it came to waking up early, I wasn't just making a passive decision. I had to put in some real effort to getting going, day after day, before this habit finally hardened into a natural instinct.

(Reflecting back for a moment, it is possible that my past served me well in terms of discipline. As a child, even though I was playful, I was a Boy Scout for a while. Then, later, as I already mentioned, I served in the army. These experiences left me with a mentality of striving to make constant self-improvement. I was always asking myself how I could be more efficient and effective. Still, however, I've probably had to struggle as much as anybody else.)

I also came to realize how much I was influenced by the people I surrounded myself with. All of us can fall into the trap of gravitating toward people who are easy to be around, who don't challenge or amplify us. This isn't to say we should only surround ourselves with wealthy or successful people, but we should be more mindful about who we're letting ourselves get close to.

Little by little, it dawned on me that when I started hanging out with more ambitious people, my own ambition level went up. But if I spent time with people who were more aimless, I began to feel softer and less positive.

*Show me who your friends are, and*
*I'll tell you who you are.*

—UNKNOWN

Going back to the game of basketball: if I put you on a court with a bunch of NBA players, even if you're the worst basketball player in the world, your game is going to get a little bit better because of the people surrounding you. You'll run a little faster; you'll jump a little higher. You will try a little bit harder.

The same applies to social media. We try to convince ourselves that social media's not entirely "real" because it's more superficial than actual socializing, but the truth is that what we do on social media has a huge impact on us. If we're following light and frivolous pages, we're going to eventually become light and frivolous people. (If we're not already!) But if we follow more inspiring and meaningful pages, then the influence they have will seep into who we are. I like to follow successful business people, positive people, funny people, great fitness gurus, talented people who inspire me, dancers who strive to get better, and more—whoever inspires me and can lead me toward a positive outcome of some kind.

When it comes to literally owning your dance floor, the trick is to not try too much at once. I've seen plenty of dancers who bite off more than they can chew. They pile on too many moves. They experiment with too many styles. But this approach goes against what I've said about infinitely improving yourself, as they're cramming the pipeline with too much material. It's not streamlined or simple. It's noisy and chaotic.

Achieving simplicity can actually be pretty complicated. The dancer who embraces and masters a lean, coherent set of moves is just like the person who's limiting his or her exposure to technology, waking up early, and surrounding him or herself with all the right people. This dancer actually owns the dance floor. This dancer makes clear choices, sets clear boundaries, and, most importantly, only tries to control what he or she knows can be controlled.

The dancer who goes for way too much—trying to levitate and fly up and touch the sun—is eventually going to burn out.

But the dancer who owns the dance floor is going to shine.

# Fast-Tempo Version

- **Choose where you dance.**
- **Practice discipline in managing your exposure to technology, other people, and other forms of influence.**
- **Remember "KISS": keep it super simple.**

# THE DANCER'S PERSONAL INSPIRATION KIT

*Your attitude, not your aptitude, will determine your altitude.*

—ZIG ZIGLAR

No dancer can keep moving without the engine of passion. No matter who you are or where you come from, if at some point you decided to dance, that means that you discovered a passion for dancing. Maybe it was the movement. Maybe it was the music. Maybe it was the desire to conquer a challenge or meet new friends or romantic partners.

Maybe it was even all of the above.

But none of those things can exist without passion. We dance because it excites us to do so. There's no such thing as a passionless dancer—unless you're talking about somebody who's been forced out onto the dance floor. As for those of us who go out there voluntarily, we're driven by a deep internal fire.

Sometimes, however, that fire goes out or feels a little lower than we're used to it feeling. We get worn down, we have to deal with various stresses, and maybe we even have a physical sickness. Those are the times when it pays to keep inspiration close at hand.

I've discussed owning your dance floor as well as the importance of keeping positive and inspirational forces around you. Here, I'd like to revisit that point from another angle, emphasizing how important it is to have positive stuff handy in case you ever need it.

Because you will!

It doesn't have to be something complicated or extreme. It can be music that you like or a good book or movie, or maybe even a book of quotations.

I'm not ashamed to admit that I have a book of inspirational quotes handy on my phone at all times. If I'm having a bad day or feeling a lack of momentum, opening up that book and reading the quotes helps me recharge my batteries. I find insights and perspectives that weren't floating through my mind just a moment earlier. Something as simple as changing my focus to the positive can have a major impact.

Investigate what makes you happy. Look around for it. Don't deprive yourself of it. You deserve to have positive things in your life. You initially made the decision to dance because it excited you; you got something from it. That's a fire worth taking good care of and tending seriously. When the flames burn lower, it's not necessarily time to throw in the towel and choose another path. More than likely, you just need to reboot yourself.

Good music, good movies, good books, good quotes—these things matter. If they didn't, we wouldn't keep on creating and buying them.

So keep the good stuff close at hand, for those days when feeling good doesn't come so easily. Think of this stuff as your own private inspiration kit. Its function is to give you a lift. You don't have to share it with anybody. In fact, you don't even have to tell anybody about it. The important thing is that you keep it handy and make sure to take it with you wherever you go.

# FAST-TEMPO VERSION

- **Create your own personal inspiration kit.**

# YOU DANCE WITH YOUR BODY—
# TREAT IT WELL!

*Early to bed and early to rise, makes a
man healthy, wealthy, and wise.*

—BENJAMIN FRANKLIN

The title of this section says it all: we're now going to spend a few moments talking about the importance of maintaining our bodies. Health and fitness are like the sun in the solar system. They are central to absolutely everything else. If they're not shining, then no light reaches anything else.

A lot of us build these little hierarchies in our minds. We say that $x$ is the most important thing to us and that $y$ is the second most important thing and so on. But I'm here to tell you that no matter who we are or what we're focused on, health and fitness should absolutely be at the top of our list of concerns.

Because if you don't have a body to dance with, then guess what? You won't get to dance!

For the longest time, health and fitness were nowhere near the forefront of my attention. As I've said, I gained a lot of weight. I was like a kid and took my health for granted. I just figured it was something that would always be there. But before I knew it, I turned around and was living in this tired, inflamed, and heavy adult body.

Things had to change.

I got into the habit of eating clean and right. I spent a couple of extra dollars on salads as opposed to French fries. And within a short span of time, I began to see that as my health profile changed, my entire life profile changed along with it.

It's just the way our minds work. When we change what's on the inside, then what's on the outside always follows.

Suddenly, the people around me were different and treated me differently as well. I felt that more people were attracted to me and not just in the literal sense of the word. My energy drew people in. It wasn't just a matter of looking or dressing better. No, it was as though my aura had suddenly been replaced and was radiating at a higher level than ever before.

Something I had long known but never fully appreciated was becoming clearer: I had to invest more in myself than I did in my job, because although my job paid my bills, only I could make a fortune.

I'm talking here about the mind and body. In other words, you alone are the instrument that makes things happen. (Or, as we like to put it in our business, "make *ship* happen!") Your job will only give back as much as you put into it.

And if you approach that job with energy, focus, excitement, enthusiasm, and joy, you can do so much more.

For me, getting up early is a huge part of my overall health and well-being.

Time and time again, I've learned that successful people I admire wake up early. There are more reasons for this than we can count. They wake up early because they want to be alone for a while. They wake up early because they're excited about what lies ahead. They wake up early because they don't want to miss anything. They hit the gym, spend time with their kids or spouse, catch up on the news, or simply get a head start on work. And on and on...

For me, the top one is that when you wake up early, you have the freedom to do what's most important to you first. The morning is generally the quietest time of the day: no phone is ringing, no e-mails are filling you inbox, and maybe you've even gotten up before anybody else in the house. That means nobody's asking you for anything and you have freedom of motion. Without any outside demands or influences, you alone can decide what you do next.

Plus, I find that I'm at my most relaxed in the morning. This could be partially biological, but it also ties in to the freedom that morning time gives me. When you're in a relaxed frame of mind, you gravitate toward self-care and investing in yourself. When you're nervous or pressured, you think about yourself less and focus on solving a particular problem. I leave that stuff for later in the day. Morning time belongs all to me. Most of my big decisions—and the good ones—I have made in the morning.

However, when you wake up late, it's harder to get a handle on your day. You're immediately bombarded by contact and issues. And you haven't even had a chance to accumulate a decent amount of energy. So you spend the whole day running behind, just waiting for another chance to sleep.

Eventually, that approach can and will completely drain you.

I go to the gym each morning. I get my blood pumping and my endorphins flowing and lay a good solid foundation for the day ahead. No matter what happens throughout the rest of the day, I know that having gone to the gym has given my body ample vitality to face it as well as I possibly can.

But going to the gym is not all I do. It depends on what I need to accomplish at the moment. Some mornings I catching up on things and get an early start on work, some mornings I spend time thinking, some mornings I read and watch TV, and some mornings are simply for family.

The first two hours of my day, which generally begins at 5:00 or 6:00 a.m., are usually the most productive. In fact, by the time most people arrive at work, I've already finished much of what I need to accomplish.

It should come as no surprise that the most successful CEOs all over the world routinely wake up and get their days started before sunrise. These are the ones who are ahead of the curve in their business practices, so it makes perfect sense that they would start their days ahead of the rest of us. Time and time again, we hear about CEOs who routinely arrive first at their offices. That's because the tone is set at the top, so by coming in early, they show that they care. And that makes all the people who work for them care that much more. My team in Miami always makes me smile when they receive e-mails from me at 8:00 or 9:00 a.m. while I'm on the West Coast, three hours behind them. They ask me, "What are you doing up so early?"

By carving out a little "me time" at the start of the day, you're sending a message to your body, mind, and spirit that you care enough to take good care of yourself. You're structuring your day in a way that puts your own well-being at the forefront, which is where it always should be. So often in our culture, we're made to feel ashamed for devoting time to ourselves, as though the act of doing so is selfish or thoughtless.

But in my opinion, without a well-oiled, highly toned, beautifully functioning self, we really can't get much done.

After I set the foundation of a healthy, fit, and energized being, I was better able than ever to attend to my ethic of constantly improving myself.

Health and fitness should not exist alone on a plateau. Like all good things, they should always be pushed in the direction of improvement.

I recall once attending a seminar where the speaker pointed out that all the cars in the parking lot were expensive and/or fancy. He then made the point that this was because successful people have the mentality of constantly wanting to make themselves better. So of course only successful people would show up to his event, while less motivated people were off kicking sand around on the beach or simply sleeping in.

Back when I was intensely involved in trading stocks, I remember one trader saying that if he lost money and just moved on, then he'd lost money. But if he lost money and studied why it was lost, then he'd just invested the "lost" money into an expensive but valuable lesson.

In other words, he desired to constantly improve.

When I do something wrong in my business, I don't let it bring me down or ignore it. Instead, I look at it like a science experiment: I study what happened and why it happened, arm myself with the information I gather, and move on.

Like a basketball player, when I miss a shot, I learn from it. Only later do I develop "selective amnesia," forgetting about it and going on to the next one. When asked if he had ever doubted he would succeed, the great Michael Jordan said no, because he had put in the work. He knew he would get there. It was simple. He had no doubt.

## Fast-Tempo Version

- **Treat your body like gold.**
- **Eat clean, stay active, and be healthy.**
- **Get up early and make your mornings count.**
- **Constantly improve!**

# BACK TO BASICS

*Don't tell me the sky's the limit when*
*there are footprints on the moon.*

—PAUL BRANDT

I started this book by talking about the basic step, and it's a completely conscious decision to now wrap things back around to this final section titled "Back to Basics."

No matter how far we go or how much we learn, it's always important to remain in touch with our basic values: health, fitness, family, loved ones, happiness, purpose, and joy.

In dancing, we always learn the basic step first, but that doesn't mean we ever leave it behind. No, it's always right there with us, an essential part of the package.

It's my hope that this book has both informed you and motivated you to take positive action. There's no use in motivating an ignorant person, as all you'll get is a motivated ignorant person. In other words, there's a huge difference between feeling motivated and actually taking action, and I sincerely hope I've played some small part in inspiring you to go after your dreams!

And as you take this positive action, always remember the following: it's not just about the destination but also about the journey.

Leave it to "the cruise guy" (which some people actually call me, by the way) to say that, right?

But it happens to be true.

And most importantly, as you get the most out of your journey, be sure you never make the mistake of leaving the basics behind.

⌣⟩

# The Butterfly Story

Day by day, we often find ourselves wishing that things would just be easier. It's common for us to get annoyed when things aren't going smoothly. Even though we might have struggled yesterday and the day before, we still act surprised when new struggles confront us, as though we're actually waiting for the day when everything will just flow.

Well, struggle is an important part of life. Indeed, it's a basic part of life, just like breathing or having a pulse. I like having fun and partying as much as the next guy, but I've learned that it's in our nature to struggle and to go through intense experiences to end up where we want to be.

Whenever I need to remind myself of this, I always turn to the butterfly story.

⌣⟩

A little boy was outside playing one day when, with great excitement, he discovered a caterpillar. Smiling, he scooped it into his hands and ran over to his mother. "One day," she told him, "it will turn into a beautiful butterfly."

The boy was beyond overjoyed to hear this. His mother told him he could keep the caterpillar until it changed into a butterfly, at which point they would set it free and watch it fly off across the sky to go live out the rest of its life.

They decided to keep the caterpillar in a small glass box. They set up a little log for it to crawl and sleep on. They regularly put in little leaves and crumbs for it to snack on. And they kept the box right beside the window, so the caterpillar had plenty of sunlight and a wonderful view to enjoy.

The boy loved having the caterpillar as his pet, but one day he noticed a problem.

The poor thing was struggling. Its body was hardening. It wasn't moving about the box any longer, and it hardly even seemed to be alive anymore.

"It's a cocoon," the boy's mother explained. "This is the shell that grows around the caterpillar before it turns into a butterfly."

The boy was fascinated but nervous. Now, every day, he watched the cocoon. Over and over again, his mother promised him that before they knew it, the cocoon would crack and out would come the butterfly they'd been waiting for.

But as excited as the boy was for that day, he didn't like to see the poor thing struggling. It looked so stuck and unhappy, turning into a thick and motionless cocoon.

One day, the boy couldn't help himself. He sneaked into the kitchen and opened the top drawer. From the drawer, he removed a slender pin.

Then, he went over to the cocoon and poked a hole through it.

Looking into the hole, he saw such glorious colors. There was a butterfly in there! Eager as ever, the boy reached into the hole and pinched a little piece of wing.

With good intentions in his heart, he pulled the butterfly out into the world.

When his mother came in and found out what had happened, she was upset, to say the least. The butterfly was having trouble moving. It flapped its wings a little, but it could not fly. Plus, its little body was swollen, for it had not had enough time to develop properly.

As the boy tried to figure out what had gone wrong, his mother took him to speak with a scientist from a local college. He learned that the butterfly had needed to struggle. Specifically, the butterfly's efforts to push its way through the cocoon's tiny opening would have moved the fluid out of its body and into its wings. But because it had been spared that struggle, the butterfly would never be able to fly. So the boy's good intentions had actually hurt the butterfly.

The boy and his mother ended up having to keep the butterfly, for it could not survive out in the world on its own.

In a way, this is a story about good parenting—allowing those in your care to develop on their own terms and not forcing them to do something before they are actually ready.

But the meaning of the story goes far beyond that.

As you go through school and life, keep in mind that struggling is an important part of any growth experience. In fact, the struggle helps you develop your ability to fly.

Going back to my own example with ADC, there were so many days when I fell into the mind-set of wanting a smoother progression. I wanted to move forward faster. I wanted to succeed right then!

However, looking back, that would not have been a good thing for me. Suppose that, in an alternate reality, an angel investor had swooped in and solved all of my problems. I never would have developed the character and business savvy required to do things all on my own.

This is why struggle, as uncomfortable as it may be, is incredibly valuable when it comes to succeeding. We shouldn't embrace struggle simply because it's natural. We should embrace struggle because we learn from it. It develops us. It hones us into who we were meant to become.

So many people hear the butterfly story and say, "Aw! That's too bad it has an unhappy ending."

But that's the whole point of the story!

A happy ending makes us feel good, but as we all know, reality doesn't consist of happy endings. Reality throws challenges and struggles at us. That doesn't mean reality is never positive. On the contrary, it's often incredibly fun and exciting.

Yet it can't always be that way. We often have to be like the butterfly inside that cocoon. The process is slow. It's difficult. It taxes our patience.

But it's also natural, essential, unavoidable, and thoroughly back to basics.

And in the end, beauty awaits!

After I started to study dancing, I learned the basics and then went up the dancing ladder: beginner, intermediate, advanced…

At the advanced level, I was itching for something new, so I scheduled a lesson with a big salsa guru. He was the most important, revered instructor out there. And I thought, "Wow! I am in for some serious lessons."

Extremely excited, I walked into the lesson. It had cost me a lot of money, but that didn't matter. This guy was worth it, based on his reputation.

I was more or less expecting some partner work. I figured the guy would have a partner on hand, whom he'd pair me up with to demonstrate some moves.

But no. It was just the two of us.

And all we worked on, for the entire time, was the basic step!

Needless to say, I was a little stunned. I thought, "What the *bleep*?"

I mean, I'd actually flown out there to see him. I'd booked a hotel, spent all this money, and there I was getting…what? The basics?

But do you know what? That man told me something that I'll never forget. He said to me, "You can never work enough on your basics."

And it just so happens to be true.

You can never improve upon your basics enough. Every time I revisit them, I discover different styles, variations, details, and nuances. And I always find myself improving on those basic moves.

It doesn't matter if you've made a million dollars, because you can always bump it up to ten million. It doesn't matter if you've traveled the world with your partner, because you can always find some new discoveries right in your own backyard.

The basics are something we can (and should) never grow out of, for they hold the center of our world together. And when our whole world's in balance, every part of it helps out every other part.

At which point, we can have truly successful and happy lives.

# Fast-Tempo Version

- **Know that struggle is a basic part of life.**
- **Know that struggle can help bring you back to basics.**
- **Keep on working on your basics.**
- **Keep on learning.**
- **Keep on growing, and** *always, always, always have fun!*

# My Personal Invitation to You

*Twenty years from now you will be more disap-*
*pointed by the things you didn't do than by the*
*ones you did do. So throw off the bowlines. Sail*
*away from the safe harbor. Catch the trade winds*
*in your sails. Explore. Dream. Discover.*

—MARK TWAIN

Well, look at this! Now you know all of these things about me, but I may not know a lot about you. If you've joined me for an ADC cruise before, then I look forward to seeing you again the next time we set sail. But if you have yet to have the ADC experience, then it's time for us to put a stop to that pitiful state of affairs.

It would be my honor and privilege to meet you in person aboard one of our ships. You will be welcomed into the ADC family and experience something that exists nowhere else upon this earth.

Call us at 877-418-3931, or contact us through our website at www. AventuraDanceCruise.com. If you use the code DanceToSuccess, you will get a fifty-dollar discount per person, as well as an oppor-tunity to have a meet-and-greet with yours truly, where I will give a short presentation and sign your copy of *Dance to Success*.

Please do not delay, as our events tend to sell out quickly. Think of all the adventures you can have with ADC. The seas await you. New friends await you.

The dance awaits you!

Moshe Rasier
a.k.a. Mr. Cruise Guy
Founder
Aventura Dance Cruise

# About the Author

Moshe A. Rasier is a highly energetic and exuberant entrepreneur, event producer, and business owner, as well as a successful investor. In 2009, he took a local dance studio global by creating the annual Aventura Dance Cruise, which in its first voyage had 472 guests before exploding to become the world's largest Latin dance cruise, with nearly 2,400 travelers in tow, selling out entire ships, and making Moshe the youngest person ever to charter a full ship for an event. Moshe uses his skills to consult other entrepreneurs and businesses in terms of marketing, investing, management, operations, and finances.

Moshe earned his MBA at Nova Southeastern University Wayne Huizenga School of Business and Entrepreneurship as well as a B.A., in Business Administration.

He is available for television, radio, and print interviews, as well as public speaking engagements.

For more information please visit:
www.AventuraDanceCruise.com
www.DanceToSuccess.com
www.MosheRasier.com